WITHDRAWN

Shelburne Farms

House, Gardens, Farm, and Barns

GLENN SUOKKO

Foreword by Alec Webb, Afterword by Megan Camp

RIZZOLI NEW YORK

New York · Paris · London · Milan

FOREWORD

Alec Webb

I was fortunate to grow up with my five siblings on Shelburne Farms. My father, Derick Webb, was the first in his family to live here year-round and actively manage the farm. As a child, when my parents still privately owned the property, I remember in the 1960s spending time around the Dairy Barn helping with chores, putting up hay for the winter, and swimming afterward in Lake Champlain. As I grew older, I became passionate about working with others on realizing a new vision for Shelburne Farms in a world facing increasing environmental degradation.

In 1972, my family started the process of transitioning Shelburne Farms to become a nonprofit organization. Today, it remains a working farm, and now, under the stewardship of its board of directors, Shelburne Farms' biggest crop is education for a sustainable future. Our vision is a healthy and just world. We strive to achieve this by working with educators who are committed to providing young people meaningful learning opportunities in their own schools and communities, locally and internationally. A large part of what we do is helping to create an educational system that uses social enterprises, farms, forests, parks, and natural areas as inspiring classrooms.

One thing that is so striking about Shelburne Farms is the dynamic combination of its natural beauty and design. The Champlain Valley's spectacular landscape is what first drew my great-grandparents, Lila and Seward Webb, to Vermont. They went on to create a working farm estate, blending natural features and majestic buildings with various agricultural and recreational activities. In the following pages Glenn Suokko provides a unique portrait in words and photographs of this remarkable place. Its historic features that stretch back to Lila and Seward's original vision in the late nineteenth century are being carefully adapted to support new uses.

There are many important aspects of Shelburne Farms that are less visible: the ideas behind it as an educational resource; the warmth and care of its community; the joy and wonder children experience here; or the constant demands of a farming way of life. It is the farmers, gardeners, craftspeople, and staff members, volunteers, and other supporters—past and present—whose work and extraordinary contributions have shaped Shelburne Farms into the place that is here today for all of us to learn from and enjoy. This book invites you to experience Shelburne Farms for yourself.

THE BEAUTY OF SHELBURNE FARMS

I will never forget my first visit to Shelburne Farms, a historic estate and farm located in northern Vermont off Lake Champlain, in the spring of 1991. The trip was to meet family and friends for dinner at the Inn at Shelburne Farms. Having just moved to Vermont from Minneapolis, I did not know much about the place. I passed through the stone-walled gate and saw meadows and pastures and came upon a magnificent barn. As I drove farther, Shelburne House, sitting boldly atop a hill, came into view. I was immediately struck by the majesty of the landscape. The scale, serenity, and beauty had a powerful affect on me. Visitors experience Shelburne Farms in many different ways. After twenty-five years, I am still discovering Shelburne Farms and always learning something from it. The excitement I felt on my first visit seems never to dissipate upon subsequent visits. It is inspiring—layered with sights, smells, sounds, tastes, and astonishing beauty.

Shelburne Farms is an idyllic pastoral place, which is also considered one of the grandest agricultural estates in America. It was envisioned by a very prestigious and influential couple, Eliza (Lila) Osgood Vanderbilt and Dr. William Seward Webb, during America's Gilded Age (1870–1898). Lila was a granddaughter of Cornelius Vanderbilt (1794–1877), the powerful railroad and transportation tycoon. Seward, the name he was commonly known by, was a highly respected doctor who left the profession to become a stockbroker on Wall Street and worked in the railroad industry for Wagner Palace Car Company, becoming its president in 1884. Lila and Seward were married in New York City in 1881.

PAGE 12

Shelburne Farms' house, gardens, farmland, barns, and woodlands are gently connected through a design conceptualized by landscape architect Frederick Law Olmsted.

OPPOSITE

Built in 1890, the Shingle-style Farm Barn, with its decorative stone and half-timber design, is today headquarters for Shelburne Farms' administrative offices and the center of its education programs.

In 1886, the Webbs hired the prominent New York City architect Robert H. Robertson and the leading landscape designer Frederick Law Olmsted to design their estate, which includes magnificent barns, greenhouses, agricultural fields, the largest domestic structure in Vermont, and a carefully considered landscape plan designed to enhance the views and enjoyment of one of the most beautiful settings in Vermont. The Webbs intended their estate to be a model agricultural farm that would promote research in crop production and how to breed livestock, as well as be a place for respite from the summer heat and the busy lives they led in New York City.

Nearly twenty years later, Lila and Seward Webb achieved their dream. The Vermont farm was never intended to be financially profitable, nor was it. Instead, it was created in the spirit of sharing scientific research, state-of-the-art farming practices, and demonstrated what nature and the land could offer through sensible cultivation and careful management. The Webbs possessed the financial means to make virtually all things possible in bringing the farm into existence, and their goal was to share the results of their discoveries. Over many years, to showcase their dream, they invited and entertained extended family, friends, social luminaries, local farmers, scientists, and politicians to experience the farm. Rather than turning agricultural products into financial reward, the Webbs cultivated the business of farming differently. Nature, the splendor of the vast landscape the Webbs had acquired, and the great rewards of living and working in the Vermont countryside were the catalysts.

Shelburne Farms was created in the nineteenth century at a time of enormous prosperity and as a result of a significant Vanderbilt legacy. When Lila's father, William Henry Vanderbilt, died in 1885, he left his daughter a substantial fortune. However, serious economic crises, the effects of two world wars, shifting tax laws, and changing societal views about the display of wealth at country estates caused them to refocus their original intent. After Seward died in 1926, and after Lila died in 1936, the next generation had to rethink what their agricultural estate was, how it needed to adapt, and what it could become. Throughout Shelburne Farms' history and over many decades of thoughtful consideration to maintain it as an agricultural estate, Shelburne Farms ultimately shifted to become a nonprofit educational organization. Its progressive evolution came about in response to economic, social, and technological changes, and a growing awareness of a new environmentalism.

By the 1960s, the Webbs' grandchildren and great-grandchildren did not have the extraordinary wealth that Lila and Seward possessed. They accepted the responsibility of redefining Shelburne Farms. The estate was in need of tremendous financial resources. The barns and infrastructure had begun to deteriorate. In 1972, rather than face dissolution, members of the Webb family established a nonprofit organization and began the journey of creating a new vision for the vast property and its buildings. With the support of extended family, close friends, and advisors, and the contributions of devoted supporters, Shelburne Farms became a dedicated organization, focusing on environmental issues, land stewardship, and sustainable agriculture. Through the implementation of an education mission, Shelburne Farms once again emerged as a forward-thinking and inspiring

OPPOSITE
Over the past forty years, Shelburne Farms has undergone an extensive program of restorations. The Formal Gardens have been restabilized and the walls, steps, balustrades, and one of two wooden pergolas (the south pergola, which was in storage for the last sixty years) have been reconstructed.

resource. The current organization maintains the progressive outlook and policies established by the Webbs, repositioning its focus "to educate for a sustainable future."

For close to a century, Shelburne Farms was a private family estate; now it is open to the public. Educators, schoolchildren, environmentalists, walkers, bird-watchers, architecture enthusiasts, restaurant diners, and curious tourists are active participants in a new Shelburne Farms. For many, it is ultimately a restorative and instructive place. Today, it remains a working farm, not unlike what Lila and Seward had originally envisioned when this enchanting setting in the late nineteenth century first captivated them. Shelburne Farms now seeks to teach and inspire sustainability practices through resource and conservation stewardship. As *Vermont Life* editor Tom Slayton aptly translated the term, "Sustainability is a practical environmentalism, akin to pastoralism, that includes human life as part of the equation. It's a new-fangled word for an old-fashioned Vermont value. The property is both a tool for teaching sustainability and a working example of that ethic and its benefits."[1] Shelburne Farms is a legible illustration of its mission. When visitors experience what it has to offer, they get that much closer to understanding the concept of sustainability and the importance of it.

In creating Shelburne Farms, Lila and Seward Webb envisioned an extremely complex estate. It went beyond what most country estates of the Gilded Age sought to do. Rather than establishing a grand country residence and focusing primarily on one area, such as raising sheep, the Webbs pursued several ventures—horse breeding; sheep, beef, and poultry production; dairy farming; crop research and development; forestry and fruit growing—and within that multiplicity sought excellence in all their endeavors. They channeled funds into each area and made them exceptional. Although in their lifetimes they had achieved due success and notoriety as the creators of a model farm, they never fully succeeded as they had hoped. Their hope for breeding the Hackney horse as a pleasure-riding and work horse, for example, ended with the advent of the combustion engine, which introduced machinery, tractors, and automobiles to do the work of horses. The Webbs had created a running faucet of financial demands and because the farm did not make a profit, declining finances became a deep concern—not severe enough to ruin the farm or family fortune—but significant enough to restrain and diminish the majority of activities. Starting in the late 1890s when Seward's health began to falter, Lila began making major reductions. Over the following decades, Shelburne Farms began its gradual decline, and the impact of the Great Depression further curtailed activities. Lila passed away in 1936, and her youngest son, Vanderbilt, took a leading role in managing the property.

In the ensuing decades, fortunately, many of Shelburne Farms' magnificent buildings were renovated, its infrastructure rebuilt, and its farmlands and landscape restored to sustainable conditions. The work is not over. Shelburne Farms today is as complex as it was in the nineteenth century, but the differentiator now is that the complexity of the parts is beneficial to the whole. Each part of Shelburne Farms is connected to the other parts, demonstrating that the agricultural and natural landscapes, the restored

OPPOSITE
Early morning sun bathes the east side of Shelburne House, which was converted into the Inn in 1987. When guests enter the Inn through the front door under the porte-cochere, they can see a bronze plaque that honors Shelburne Farms as a National Historic Landmark, designated by the National Park Service in 2001.

buildings and infrastructure, and the nonprofit organization that propels them are the channels for the education resources it creates. The magnificent barns are now learning spaces for schoolchildren and for educators who come from around the world to study conservation principles. Children are inspired by what they discover and motivate their families and friends. Educators take that learning back to their own classrooms to influence their community.

Shelburne House, the stunning home that Lila and Seward built for their family, was eventually converted into an inn, where guests are now able to immerse themselves in the history of an American story and benefit from the clean air, land, spectacular views, and respite that staying at the Inn offers. The Inn and several on-campus houses are also used as the residences for visiting educators, researchers, and conservationists. "Farm-to-table" and "garden-to-plate" does not get much closer than it does at Shelburne Farms. The fruit and vegetables that its Vegetable Garden grows and the meat and dairy that its Dairy Farm raises are the wholesome, honest ingredients that feed guests in its own restaurant at the Inn, its food cart, and at special events held around the property. Hundreds of acres of fertile pasturelands are the home to grazing Brown Swiss cows; the milk they produce is turned into Cheddar cheese that is sold on the property and all over the country. Maple syrup, made in late winter from the sap that flows from hundreds of maple trees on the fourteen-acre "sugarbush," is another of its revered food products.

In 2001, Shelburne Farms was designated a National Historic Landmark by the National Park Service. National Historic Landmarks are nationally significant historic places designated because they possess exceptional value or quality in illustrating or interpreting the heritage of the United States.[2] Just over 2,500 sites have received this national distinction; for example, the White House in Washington, D.C., Monticello in Virginia, John and Priscilla Alden Family Sites in Massachusetts, the Empire State Building in New York, and Fort Yellowstone in Idaho.

When Lila and Seward Webb's descendants transformed Shelburne Farms from a private estate to a nonprofit educational resource open to the public, they saved the spirit of a family legacy. Otherwise, this vast parcel of land might have become irrevocably split up and commercially or privately developed. The nonprofit organization is led by a new generation of supporters who carefully guide it forward. After decades of restoration of the property's greatest assets—Shelburne House and its Formal Gardens; the Farm, Breeding, and Coach barns; the landscape design; and the Dairy Farm and Vegetable Garden—their purpose has been redefined and aligned with contemporary issues of land use.

Today, the clear-pitched voices of happy children—calling out, sharing discoveries—are the promising sounds that resonate outside the Farm Barn, the education epicenter of Shelburne Farms. The children might be students on a school field trip or visiting with their families. Adding to this vibrant enthusiasm are the delightful sounds of chickens clucking, lambs bleating, calves braying, and a cow mooing. To complete this picture is the warmth of the sun; a gentle, cool breeze off Lake Champlain; and the sweet smell of meadow wildflowers. Watch the herd of Brown Swiss

OPPOSITE
Shelburne Farms is well known for its magnificent barns, house, and vast, pristine pasturelands.

cows meandering its way across the pastures, dozens of sheep resting contentedly under the shade of a big, old oak tree, the green grass swaying in the fields, and look above to a soft, blue sky, dotted with pure-white puffy clouds. The impression the visitor is left with is the beauty and simplicity of the natural environment that this remarkable family and many supporters have worked tirelessly to create.

Walk in any direction—along a gravel road, up a hill, on a trail through the woods—and you begin to hear the melody of nature and the landscape's music, from rustling leaves and chirping crickets to cawing crows, and a farm tractor at work in the distance. Around the corner, the vast open space over Lake Champlain to the west is awe-inspiring, and beyond that are the magnificent and layered, often hazy, silhouettes of the mighty Adirondack Mountains. Turn around completely to the east and the gentle peaks of the Green Mountains emerge. It is hard to not draw a deep breath.

Shelburne Farms is unlike any historic or contemporary property in America. Stone Barns Center for Food and Agriculture, just twenty-five miles north of Manhattan, in Pocantico Hills, New York, is similar in concept. That property, donated by David Rockefeller and his family in the 1990s, is a working farm and a nonprofit educational organization dedicated to creating healthy, sustainable food systems. It also operates a restaurant in partnership with Blue Hill that serves food made from ingredients raised or grown on the property. But the beauty and vast landscape of Shelburne Farms is perhaps more analogous to agricultural regions in rural, Alpine Switzerland that maintain a strong commitment to dairy cows and making cheese, or the Lake District in England, a region known for raising fine-quality sheep breeds. In both communities, the synthesis of majestic mountains, vast pasturelands, historic buildings, agricultural endeavors, and the products of those activities provide a viable framework for localized agricultural, cultural, and economic sustainability.

Today, Shelburne Farms' mission continues the philosophical foundations of its founders, Lila and Seward Webb—to create a working landscape and farm devoted to innovation and learning as much as to the enjoyment of nature. The original structures are a physical reminder of the ambition, taste, and lifestyle of this progressive couple. They are also symbols of a love for living in the country and of country ways of life. If the house, gardens, barns, and landscape that the Webbs created did not exist today, the experience would be quite different for anyone visiting Shelburne Farms. It is hard to imagine it without its magnificent barns, without its grand house, without its pastures and woodlands, without its walking trails, and without its magnificent mountain and lake views. Fortunately, Shelburne Farms remains vital. And through its history, this great property tells an important story, one that is multilayered and preserved for generations to come. It is a living example of sustainability.

LAND AND LAKE

The magnificence of Shelburne Farms owes much of its distinctive character to the beauty of its natural setting. Shelburne Farms is well situated on the eastern shore of Lake Champlain, the large body of water that separates the border between Vermont and New York. The lake flows north and joins the Richelieu River in Quebec, which connects to the Saint Lawrence River and eventually empties into the Atlantic Ocean. To the east are Vermont's gentle Green Mountains. To the west are New York's monumental Adirondack Mountains. Shelburne Farms lies in the middle of the two mountain ranges, hugging the rugged shoreline and rocky inlets of the lake.

The view of the Green Mountains is best observed from the eastern pastures, the Farm Barn, and most dramatically from the hill behind the Farm Barn. The iconic silhouette of Camel's Hump heightens the softness and tranquility of Vermont's pastoral landscape. Lake Champlain is often as blue as the ocean; it reflects the skies above it. On a misty day, when visibility of the New York shore is absent, the lake appears to be an endless sea. At its widest distance, fourteen miles of water separate the two states. From Shelburne, the New York shore and Adirondack Mountains that rise behind it feel far away. The impressive views of Lake Champlain and Adirondack Park are a significant part of the character of Shelburne Farms. The broadest view to the west can be seen from atop Lone Tree Hill, which at one time had been cleared of most of its trees, offering uninterrupted, panoramic views to the eastern and western mountain ranges.

The fourteen-hundred acres that comprise Shelburne Farms today are among the most fertile in Vermont. It was here where, due to the rich soil

PAGES 24–25

Viewed from one of Shelburne Farms' many pastures, Shelburne House is beautifully sited atop a hill against the dramatic backdrop of New York's Adirondack Mountains. Lake Champlain divides a large portion of the border between the two states. At its widest point just north of Shelburne Farms, the lake measures fourteen miles across from Vermont to New York.

BELOW

A 1900 photograph taken from the hill on the northeastern side of Shelburne House shows the state-of-the-art "Macadam" road meandering along the lake and around "Elm Tree Swamp." In 1820, Scottish engineer John Loudon McAdam created the method of laying crushed stone in compact layers to provide a smooth surface for coach and carriage riding. Frederick Law Olmsted proposed a landscape plan for travel through the estate's property that was gentle and organic, offering beautiful views of the Farms' natural and man-made features. The property remains much the same today as it was conceived in the nineteenth century.

OPPOSITE

From the property's eastern pastures, views of Vermont's gentle, rolling hills culminate with the Green Mountains, a 250-mile portion of the Appalachian Mountains that runs south to north through Vermont. The iconic Camel's Hump is the range's third-highest mountain and most renowned peak. It is a protected area and was designated as a U.S. National Natural Landmark in 1968.

conditions, early European settlers chose to work the land and build lives from the products of their efforts. Their activities began the transformation of a former unspoiled, wild natural resource used by Native Americans for hunting into a managed landscape. After Lila and Seward Webb acquired dozens of individual farms for Shelburne Farms, they embarked on a massive plan to create one magnificent model estate farm—often thought of as an "ornamental" farm, due to the extraordinary farm and domestic architecture, park-like landscape, and considerable attention to sophisticated design on every level. The landscape was intended for agricultural use, but the Webbs also wished to preserve natural woodlands and to offer opportunities for pleasure activities such as horseback and carriage riding, and what was a relatively new sport at the time—golf.

Robert H. Robertson, who was the chief architectural designer of Shelburne House and the Farm, Coach, and Breeding barns, "invited landscape architect Frederick Law Olmsted to oversee the design of the estate landscape."[3] Olmsted is generally thought of as the father of landscape architecture in America, well known for his design of Central Park in New York City and Boston's Emerald Necklace, as well as for numerous urban public parks and university campuses across the country and in Canada. An early leader of the conservation movement in the late nineteenth century, he advocated the preservation of important natural sites such as Niagara Falls and the greater Adirondack Mountains region. He laid the philosophical foundation for the National Park System. Through his public and private commissions, he set the standard of design excellence in preserving

The 1927 aerial view of Shelburne House, its Formal Gardens, and park landscape shows the residential buildings and some of the recreational areas of the property's landscape design. The land between the lake and the semicircular garden space was eventually lost, due to erosion. The stone balustrade was threatened and a portion of it collapsed and fell into the lake. In 2007, as a result of a major gift to restore the Formal Gardens, the land was reinstated, the balustrade rebuilt, and the magnificent portion of the gardens restored to its former grandeur.

OPPOSITE
Shelburne House was built on a former hillside apple orchard. Its auspicious siting and architectural scale make it a commanding and stately force that can be seen from various points on the property and from Lake Champlain. The flat area (far right) was the first tee for the golf links course.

and enhancing the beauty of nature within a carefully considered design construct consisting of roadways, walkways, open spaces, and plantings. "Olmsted saw landscape as a powerful method of social improvement that could provide refreshment and solace to Americans who were increasingly detached from nature, as the nation became more and more urbanized."[4]

Olmsted embarked on designing a landscape plan for the Webb's entire property that included building sites, roadways, pastures, natural areas, hayfields, carriage and riding trails, and open spaces. Functionality is a significant component of landscape design, and as a complement to practicality, Olmsted sought to enhance aesthetic experience by providing carefully considered views. "Like the parkways that Olmsted had designed for many of his public park commissions, the drives skirted the edges of the fields and woodlands, provided glimpses of the estate buildings, the lake, and the mountains to heighten the anticipation of wide vistas, and met in triangular junctions rather than at right angles."[5] The Webbs, however, hesitated to make a commitment to aspects of Olmsted's plan. The concepts for houses that Olmsted had sited and Robertson had designed would have been at an enormous cost. Olmsted had also developed a concept for an arboretum that the Webbs could not commit to. As it turned out, the Webbs were not willing to implement Olmsted's full vision for Shelburne Farms. "Olmsted was quite likely discouraged and frustrated by Seward and Lila's disregard for his advice. He began to disengage himself from the Shelburne Farms project, first turning it over to other members of his firm and then ceasing to work on it altogether around 1889."[6]

BELOW

Fox hunting was a popular activity at the turn of the twentieth century, and the Shelburne Farms' property was an ideal mix of open and forested land populated by miles of trails that made riding on horseback perfect for this sport. Foxhounds were bred on the property, and several period photographs suggest that many elaborate riding parties were organized for autumn hunts.

OPPOSITE

Of the total 1,400 acres that comprise Shelburne Farms today, approximately three hundred acres are used for animal pastures, six hundred as hayfields and open land for feed, three hundred as managed woodlands, and seven for vegetable gardens.

PAGE 32

The Webbs were active sportsmen on land and on water. They owned several boats; among them were three yachts that they sailed on the vast open waters of Lake Champlain. Shown in the 1902 photograph on the *Elfrida II* (top) are Lila (center), her two sons, Vanderbilt and James Watson, and her daughter, Frederica (far right). The photograph below it shows the crew on board the *Elfrida I*, which was in use between 1889 and 1898, docked in the cove at Shelburne Farms.

PAGES 33–59

The Shelburne Farms landscape is a composition of pastoral beauty that unifies open land, woodlands, and lake throughout the seasons. Miles of gravel roadways, trails, and paths link many of its parts so that individuals can experience its natural magnificence.

Olmsted's original concept, however, was later followed by the Webbs' longtime farm manager Archibald Taylor, who developed the landscape and grounds of the estate, implementing the major structural concepts that Olmsted had wished to execute. Ultimately, the nineteenth-century vision serves as a structural overlay for Shelburne Farms' working landscape today. At the root of Olmsted's plan was the integration and enhancement of connectivity between three major areas of activity: farm and agricultural land, natural spaces and woodlands, and residential and recreational areas. This organizational scheme is as important today as it was at its inception.

An important part of the connection between the former Gilded Age estate and the present organization is the preservation of the landscape and structures. During the restoration, several essential landscape features were improved with the stabilization of the eroding lakeshore at the Formal Gardens, the protection of natural areas for indigenous and seasonal migrating wildlife, forest revitalization, and the replanting of trees along the roadways.

Olmsted believed that nature refreshes the body and mind; his parks were designed to allow the viewer to appreciate the salubrious effects of the natural world. Today, the organization encourages exploring Shelburne Farms' landscape on foot rather than driving through it. Inaccessible by car, miles of well-maintained trails link the farmlands, buildings, woodlands, and lake together. Discovering the property at a more intimate pace, walkers and hikers can absorb the sheer beauty of nature along the way and experience it more fully.

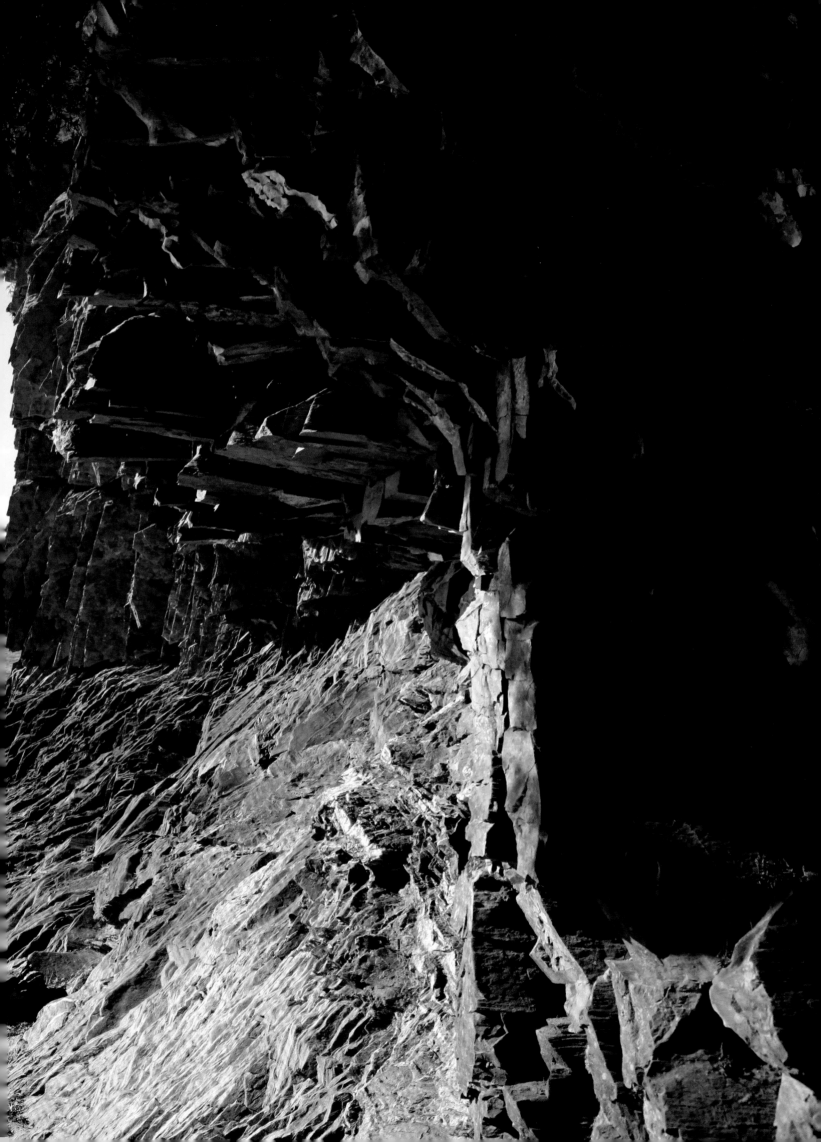

SHELBURNE HOUSE

During the late nineteenth century, the Vanderbilts were the leaders in creating new residential sensations and some of the most opulent mansions in the United States. Lila Webb's siblings began to build "country cottages" as summer retreats outside of New York City in fashionable settings such as Newport, Rhode Island, and Lenox, Massachusetts. The architectural inspiration for Lila's brother William's fifty-room Marble House in Newport was inspired by the Petit Trianon at the Palace of Versailles in France. The Breakers, created by Lila's brother Cornelius Vanderbilt II, was designed in an imposing Italianate Renaissance style and is the largest mansion in Newport. These houses, and others like them, were the residential manifestations of immense wealth and social ambition in a time known as the Gilded Age, which lasted roughly from 1870 to 1898. In England, this time period is known as the Victorian era, and in France, as the Belle Époque. On the East Coast of the United States, some wealthy Americans sought to showcase their sumptuous taste and, in aspiring to live like European aristocracy, were determined to build houses like them. Lila, the eighth child and youngest daughter of William Henry Vanderbilt, and her husband, Dr. William Seward Webb, chose to construct their country estate not in the fashionable locations of the day but in rural Vermont. Its great natural beauty, far away from the social strictures and demands of their social status, captivated them.

A passage in Seward's journal in the summer of 1879 conveys his passion for Lake Champlain and Vermont: "I wanted my Lila to see it all & the scenery was beautiful. You know it is one of the loveliest lakes in the East.

PAGES 62–63

At far right, the east facade of Shelburne House, 1900. At far left, the original Coach Barn, which dates from 1888; it was demolished and a new Coach Barn was built in its place in 1901.

MAIN HALL

PAGE 64

Detail of the stained-glass window by Arnold & Locke, Brooklyn, New York, 1887.

PAGE 65

The vestibule of the main hall where the Webbs received guests over a century ago and where today Inn guests first enter the house. The table and chairs were moved from the Webbs' New York City residence to Shelburne House in 1913.

BELOW, LEFT

The details of the oak wall, mantel carvings, and tile-faced fireplace in the main hall illustrate the harmonious complexity of varied designs.

BELOW, RIGHT

The Webbs brought skilled craftsmen from New York City to Shelburne to create the ornately carved woodwork and marble work throughout the house. They stayed in boarding houses on the property. The Kodiak bear in bronze on the mantel is by an unknown artist.

OPPOSITE

The dark, heavily carved cabinet with a stained-glass door complements the quartered-oak wall paneling in the public room off the main hall.

The bold sharp Adirondacks in the West, which are grand, and the Green Mountains in the East. The Lake is full of islands on any one of which I would like to spend a month with my wife, where we could be all alone, away from all trouble, no one to disturb us, oh how happy we would be."[7] Not far from Burlington, Vermont, where the Webbs had briefly established a residence, they ultimately settled on creating an estate and working farm in Shelburne.

Shelburne House, the retreat that Lila and Seward created, was built between 1887 and 1899 in several stages, but it is different in style and quite modest compared to the Beaux-Arts–style mansions of their wealthy contemporaries. Beaux-Arts, the neoclassical architectural style rooted in the Paris design academia, widely influenced civic and domestic architecture in the United States; the White House in Washington, D.C., is among the many fine residential examples. Lila and Seward aimed to build a country house that was in keeping with the fashion of the day, so they hired successful New York City architect Robert H. Robertson, a prolific designer of commercial, residential, and public institutions throughout the eastern United States. He was well versed in all the popular architectural styles of the day—Victorian Gothic, Richardsonian Romanesque, Shingle, Queen Anne, and Classical Revival. Robertson designed several schemes for this commission, from an extravagant residence that he proposed for a site on the property known as Lone Tree Hill that included a design similar in style to the White House to a massive, medieval-style stone fortress inspired by Warwick Castle in England. In 1893, Lila and Seward rejected Robertson's

MAIN HALL

BELOW, LEFT

Lila and Seward's son, James Watson Webb, a left-handed polo and golf player, is photographed about to tee off from the first tee of the nine-hole Shelburne Farms Links, circa 1915–20. Sporting activities, such as golf and horseback riding, were an important part of the social life at Shelburne Farms. The links course design is attributed to Scottish golfer Willie Park Jr. (1864–1925).

BELOW, RIGHT

Electra Havemeyer Webb, wife of James Watson Webb, on horseback on the property, circa 1909. In 1947, Electra founded the Shelburne Museum—thirty-nine distinctive structures on forty-five acres located a few miles from Shelburne Farms that showcases New England architecture, American folk art, and French Impressionist paintings.

OPPOSITE

Over the rose-colored marble fireplace with its oak mantel are companion prints by the German publisher Friedrich Bruckmann of the English Romantic poet Lord Byron and German literature luminary Johann Christoph Friedrich von Schiller. A deer in bronze by Antoine-Louis Barye (1796–1875), left, balances the bronze Kodiak bear, right.

designs of a massive residence in favor of developing and enlarging the temporary house Robertson had previously built for them on the point overlooking Lake Champlain. On a hilltop apple orchard, the couple created a home that was more informal and personal in scale than their original opulent intentions; however, it was still the largest domestic structure built in Vermont at the time.

Beginning in 1893, Shelburne House was reconfigured, expanded, and transformed to become a three-story residence consisting of private spaces for the Webb family, service areas, public rooms, and guest rooms for the many visitors Lila and Seward would graciously entertain. Robertson designed the house in a combination of Elizabethan Revival and Shingle styles, the latter a popular architectural style of the era that had its roots in English design, combined with a new interest in New England Colonial architecture. Wealthy contemporaries who were not building summer "cottages" as bold and lavish as Lila's brothers were developing in Newport often chose the amalgamated English-American Shingle style for their summer or seaside homes in other affluent places such as Manchester-by-the-Sea, Massachusetts, and East Hampton, Long Island. Lila's sister, Emily Vanderbilt Sloane, created Elm Court in Lenox, Massachusetts, which is the largest Shingle-style house in the United States. The remodeled Shelburne House exhibited the luxury that Lila and Seward were accustomed to, while at the same time it was an expression of the comfort that ideally suited their lifestyle in Vermont. Shelburne House was quite different from the Gilded Age homes in vogue in Newport—it is an articulation of

TEA ROOM

BELOW

The Tea Room is at the intersection of the original house, built in 1888, and the new wing that was added a decade later. It served as the Webbs' temporary dining room until the Marble Dining Room was completed in 1900. This elegant space, with its decorative boxed ceiling and classical arched doorways, became both a passageway and a living space known as a Corridor Hall. Today, it is the room at the Inn where guests are served tea in the afternoon or socialize over cocktails before dinner.

OPPOSITE

In the Tea Room hangs *Mrs. Ralph Pulitzer*, a 1904 portrait of Lila and Seward's daughter, Frederica, by the painter Benjamin C. Porter (1845–1908), who maintained studios in Boston and New York City. The American Empire–style sideboard, dating from 1815 to 1840, is a companion to the sideboard that is pictured in the period photograph below.

PAGE 72

A circa-1889 portrait of Lila Webb by New York City–society portrait painter George Chickering Munzig (1859–1908).

PAGE 73

Over the mantel is a lithograph portrait of Lila's grandfather, Cornelius Vanderbilt, the American business magnate who built his wealth in railroads and shipping.

the Webbs' personal taste and style. The interiors were—and still are—an eclectic mix of many styles and influences.

The Webb family spent winters in New York City, where they had a sumptuous residence on Fifth Avenue. They moved to Shelburne, often full-time from May to October, as well as for periodic visits throughout the year and on holidays. Typical of the period and the Victorian style the Webbs embraced, the rooms of the house were decorated with massive furnishings, overstuffed sofas, artwork, books, family portraits and photographs, rich fabrics, and decorative wallpapers. Celebrating the custom of the day to spend long periods of summertime in the countryside, Lila and Seward invited extended family and friends to join them and to stay in the house's sixteen capacious guest rooms, each uniquely decorated in a diversity of styles ranging from French Empire and Louis XVI to seventeenth-century Dutch and Colonial Revival. Lila and Seward hosted sumptuous dinner parties in the formal neoclassical Marble Dining Room, where their house staff served guests, seated at a seventeen-foot-long mahogany table, several courses of French cuisine and fine wines.

The house enjoyed decades of private use by Lila and Seward's descendants, but slowly parts of the structure began to slip into decline. Damage due to the long, harsh winters combined with the unrelenting financial demands for the upkeep of such a large house in the twentieth century required the family and later the nonprofit Shelburne Farms' board of trustees to make hard decisions about the building. Some of its original features, including the glass conservatory joined to the dining room and

EAST DINING ROOM

BELOW

After the original house was renovated in 1895, the former servants' hall became Seward Webb's office, where he conducted business with farm managers and his secretary from his New York City office. The densely decorated room shown in the photograph from 1900 was filled with books and taxidermied game heads. Seward's mahogany desk is still on the property, used in Shelburne Farms' administrative offices.

OPPOSITE

During the 1985–87 restoration of Seward Webb's office, the room's architectural features were beautifully refurbished. Today, this spacious room is used for private dinners and for meetings held for visiting educators and nonprofit organizations. Seward was keenly interested in the weather and tracking winds; his anemometer is today installed over the mantel, which is connected to a weathervane on the roof directly overhead.

the entire servants' wing, were eventually removed. Parts of the house were boarded up, altered, and repurposed. Later, leaking roofs caused considerable water damage to the interior rooms, wallpapers, furnishings, and floors. Some of the furnishings and artwork were dispersed among family members or sold at auction. As the private estate transitioned to become a nonprofit organization in the 1970s, plans to restore the house were underway. A combination of foundation grants and charitable gifts provided the organization with the capacity to recreate Shelburne House for a new era. Starting in 1985, Shelburne House went through a major and sensitive two-year restoration, which revealed many of the original architectural and decorative features. Over half of the original furnishings and objects were restored or returned and placed in or around their original settings.

Shelburne House opened to the public in 1987, not as a museum, but as the Inn at Shelburne Farms. The Inn is open seasonally, from May to October. It welcomes overnight guests, who, while staying in one of the twenty-four guest rooms, can enjoy the comfort and ease of the entire house as well as explore the vast property. When it was built, Shelburne House was considered a state-of-the-art residence; it was wired for electricity throughout the house and "modern" plumbing was introduced into all twenty-three of its bathrooms. Many of the beautiful old fixtures remain. The amenities of the present century, such as television and air conditioning in every room, have purposely not been installed. Historic character endures in the house and the experience is that of being a guest in a bygone era.

EAST DINING ROOM

LEFT

The door knocker outside Seward's office at Shelburne House. The location of his office allowed him to conduct business by admitting associates and visitors directly into it; they did not have to enter the house and interrupt the family's privacy.

BELOW

The south side of Shelburne House, circa 1900. Visitors entered the main house through a Dutch door under the porte-cochere. Visitors seeking Seward on business matters entered his office from a separate door beyond the porte-cochere.

OPPOSITE

A detail of the fireplace mantel in the private meeting and dining room, formerly Seward Webb's office.

LIBRARY

BELOW, LEFT

Seward's personal bookplate depicts the Webb family crest, with the motto *Principia Non Homines* (Principles Not Men). Many of the books in the library that contain Seward's bookplate are inscribed from him to Lila.

BELOW, RIGHT

Lila's personal bookplate includes a drawing of the interior of the library, illustrating the large picture window on the west side of the room with views of her Formal Gardens, Lake Champlain, and New York's Adirondack Mountains.

OPPOSITE

More than six thousand volumes formed the collection of books in the Webbs' library, most of which are still in place in the room or stored in the archives of the house. Many of the books are beautifully bound in leather with gold stamping and marbleized endpapers. To convey a sense of classical antiquity in the room, three marble busts by unknown artists—of a woman, Medusa, and the young Emperor Augustus—remain in their original places on top of the bookshelves.

In 2001, the Shelburne Farms' property received the high honor of becoming a National Historic Landmark. A bronze plaque is proudly displayed on the wall outside the front door of the Inn. It states:

This site possesses national historical significance in commemorating the history of the Untied States of America. This is one of the finest examples in the nation of a late 19th–20th century model farm and country estate, created by Dr. William Seward and Lila Vanderbilt Webb. The estate is noted for its exemplary agricultural, architectural, and landscape design achievements.

Such landmarks are nominated and chosen by the National Park Service to convey our proud American heritage. In this highly technological age, it is essential to retain examples of our agrarian, architectural, and socioeconomic history, in which Shelburne Farms blends so magnificently. Shelburne House is one of the major buildings on the property that has endured. It is a connection to a significant past with forward-thinking goals.

LIBRARY

LEFT

The library is located in the public area of the house between the main receiving hall and the south porch. It was designed to be an informal living space for reading and conversation. Today, the same low sofas and several upholstered chairs provide Inn guests with choices of comfortable places to sit.

BELOW

The library contains about eighty percent of its original furnishings: reading tables, chairs, sofas, side tables, and benches. Most of the sumptuous chairs have been reupholstered. The chair pictured is covered in "Falk Manor House," a silk and velvet fabric by Scalamandré.

OPPOSITE

Lila Webb was an avid reader and is alleged to have read many of the books in the library. Subjects vary and include literature, art, philosophy, history, science, poetry, and more.

LIBRARY

LEFT, BOTTOM, AND OPPOSITE
The green marble mantel is carved with leaf and flower patterns that are also present throughout the library on several wooden columns, ceiling trim, and bookshelves. The blue-green paint is original to the room, a color that is matched or complemented in many of the upholstery fabrics.

CORRIDOR HALL

In the late 1950s, Webb family members affectionately named Corridor Hall "no man's land." During the 1940s and 1950s, two Webb families lived in the house and the long hallway was "neutral territory" between the two separate households, one on the south side of the house and the other on the north side.

LEFT

In the corridor between the Tea Room and Marble Dining Room stands a stately English eighteenth-century "grandfather" clock, decorated in japanning, a popular technique of the time that mimicked the look of Eastern lacquerware.

BELOW

The photograph from 1900 shows Corridor Hall decorated with sumptuous fabrics, oriental rugs, curio cabinets, artwork, and potted palms. Seen through the open doorway of the Marble Dining Room is a Chippendale-style mahogany dining chair.

OPPOSITE

In the original layout of the house, the temporary dining room and Corridor Hall were divided into a kitchen, breakfast room, butler's pantry, and service hallway. During the 1899–1900 renovation, walls were removed to open the space for living and to create a grand processional walkway to the formal dining room. The more formal style included the making of classical arches, coffered ceilings, and decorative moldings.

CORRIDOR HALL

LEFT

Dating from 1842 and bearing the Webb name, the bottle of Madeira is one of the many treasures visitors to the Inn can discover. Madeira was a popular European export alcohol in the nineteenth century because it, unlike wine, does not spoil as easily with age or fluctuation in temperature, as could happen with wine on long voyages across the ocean.

BELOW, LEFT AND RIGHT

A few of the delicate gold-rimmed teacups and saucers and silver flatware place settings, engraved with the Webb family crest, remain in the Shelburne House collections. Much of the silver, china, and decorative objects were dispersed among family members after Lila Webb's death in 1936.

OPPOSITE

The Corridor Hall and the Tea Room were decorated in the early 1900s. The blue and silvery-green classical-design wallpaper is original, purchased from F. R. Beck and Company, in New York City, and one of three original wall coverings that remain in the house.

MARBLE DINING ROOM

The Marble Dining Room is perhaps the most formal room in the house. Added as part of a wing during the 1899–1900 renovations, the impressive room was the epicenter of lavish entertaining. An early printed menu in the Shelburne House collections illustrates that guests were often served French-style meals consisting of several courses: 1. Consommé des Mages; 2. Saumon Poché et Sauce Hollandaise, Salade de Tomates et Concombres; 3. Dindonneau à la Brioche, Saucisses, Cranberry Jelly, Pommes Rissolées, Choux-fleurs Polonaise; 4. Mousse de Jambon, Royale; and 5. Grousse dorée sur Canapé, Pommes en Liard, Salad Alexandra.

BELOW

Many features of the original 1900 Marble Dining Room remain today: wall coverings, sculptures, floor lamps, and sideboard. The photograph from 1902 shows the dining room with its second set of dining table and chairs of neoclassical design, which are now used in the private dining and meeting room at the Inn. To the left is the original Conservatory, a magnificent semicircular glass room that was leaking and in disrepair. In the early 1940s it was removed and the opening to it filled in with a brick wall.

OPPOSITE

The massive white marble sideboard, clay pots (originally from the Formal Gardens), and *torchères* are original to the dining room, as is the black-and-white-patterned marble floor; the white marble is from Vermont. Over the sideboard hangs a portrait of Seward Webb, painted in 1886 by New York City artist James Carroll Beckwith (1852–1917).

MARBLE DINING ROOM

LEFT

The dining room features an ornate plaster ceiling with classical acanthus-leaf designs, installed by skilled craftsmen from New York City, who came to Vermont by train to work on the house.

BELOW, LEFT AND RIGHT

Lighting in the dining room includes several bronze *torchères* with beaded lamp coverings, made by Edward F. Caldwell & Company, New York City, who also provided light fixtures for the White House in Washington, D.C., the Andrew Carnegie residence in New York City, and the Frederick W. Vanderbilt House in Hyde Park, New York. A copy of a Roman bronze statue stands on a marble column outside the former entryway to the Conservatory.

OPPOSITE

The rich red-and-crimson silk damask wall coverings lend a sense of stately elegance to the Marble Dining Room. A mahogany side chair is one of two original chairs that remain today. The famous French portrait painter Jules Joseph Lefebvre (1836–1911) completed the portrait of Lila Vanderbilt, wearing a red silk sash, in 1880 in Paris. The white marble baseboards are from stone, quarried in Vermont.

GAME ROOM

LEFT

Hunting was a popular activity among the upper classes during the decades before and after the turn of the nineteenth century. An American bald eagle is one of the Webbs' many game trophies on display in the Game Room. Later, the Bald Eagle Protection Act of 1940 was enacted to protect the species. American bald eagles are often sighted over the property today.

BELOW

The photograph from circa 1900 shows the Game Room—or the "north room" as it was called during Lila and Seward's era—furnished with much of the furniture that remains in the room today. It was here that, presumably, male family members and guests convened after dinner for cigars and a game of billiards. The Game Room is easily accessible through a door in the north corner of the dining room. The guest bedrooms above the room were where the male guests often stayed.

OPPOSITE

The stones for the massive sandstone fireplace came from across the lake in Potsdam, New York. Today, oriental rugs have replaced the former animal skins.

GAME ROOM

LEFT
The circa-1890 photograph of William Seward Webb in his buffalo coat and buffalo cap was taken on the south porch, outside the Library.

BELOW LEFT, BELOW RIGHT, AND OPPOSITE
The Game Room is full of massive oak tables and Elizabethan Revival furniture with intricate carved surfaces with portraits, figures, and decorations that the Webbs had moved from their New York City residence. The 1898 billiard table by Brunswick-Balke-Collender Company takes center stage. Iron ceiling lighting fixtures by Edward F. Caldwell & Company and wall bracket lighting with beaded lamp coverings by the same maker illuminate the romantic room. Beautiful stained-glass windows fill the room with a natural, raking light that casts a green glow throughout the day and complement the green surface of the billiard table.

GAME ROOM

LEFT

A monumental seventeenth-century linen chest—used for storing textiles, clothing, sheets, and other fabrics—from the Webbs' New York City residence was reinstalled along a wall of the Game Room. In front of it are a table and set of leather upholstered chairs with Moroccan-carved themes, also from the New York City residence.

BELOW, LEFT

A detail of the front doors of the intricately carved seventeenth-century linen chest includes profiles of illustrious personalities whose names are now lost to history.

BELOW, RIGHT

The decorative detail of a mythological hybrid creature is also a structural feature to the cabinet and chest of drawers.

OPPOSITE

An Elizabethan Revival oak armchair, built by an unknown maker, resides in a corner below the trophy head of an American bison. The oak wall paneling, elaborately carved table, and the equally impressive armchairs by its side reflect the furnishing designs and decorating sensibilities of the Gilded Age. These furnishings, transitioned from New York City to Vermont, were vastly different from the austere, light, country-style furniture that was produced at the time.

BEDROOMS

LEFT AND BELOW

When it was completed in 1900, Shelburne House was considered a very modern home. Behind-the-scenes technology provided the family and its guests with many amenities that were not widely common in most Vermont houses. In every room of Shelburne House, single, double, or triple diamond-shaped brass plates with ivory buttons (below) allowed family and guests to summon household staff to attend to an individual's needs. Although no longer in working order, these service bells have been preserved to illustrate the social history of the era. The panel (left) alerted household staff of the room in the house where attention was needed.

OPPOSITE

The second-floor landing's seating area is at the intersection between the Webb family's bedrooms and the hall of guest bedrooms. It is decorated in a red-on-white printed reproduction wallpaper whose pattern mimics the original flocked wallpaper. It was donated by Old Deerfield Fabrics of New Jersey for the 1985–87 restoration. Red wall-to-wall carpeting adds another sumptuous layer to the second- and third-floor bedroom halls, while quieting the footsteps of individuals walking through this area.

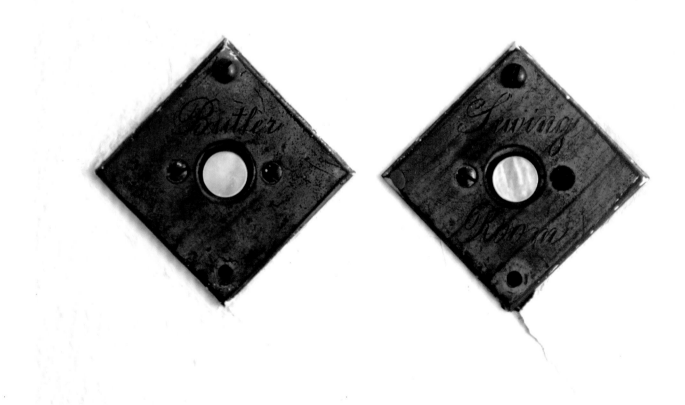

BEDROOMS

LEFT

A photograph of an 1889 oil painting by George Munzig (1859–1908) of Lila and her son, James Watson Webb. The original portrait is in the Shelburne Museum collection.

BELOW

Lila's bedroom as it was decorated in 1900.

OPPOSITE

Today, Lila's bedroom is an Inn guest room; most of the original furnishings remain, including chairs, large armoires, and the wall sconces and chandelier.

PAGE 102, TOP LEFT

Seward Webb's bedroom contains several original furnishings, including Seward's bed, dresser, clock, and fire screen. Over the mantel is a portrait of his father, General James Watson Webb (1802–1884).

PAGE 102, TOP RIGHT

A photograph of Seward Webb, circa 1904, by the Falk Studio, New York City. The wallpaper in the room is a reproduction from Zoffany, the wallcovering company headquartered in England, of the "Pimpernel" wallpaper designed by William Morris in 1876 for his dining room at Kelmscott House, London.

PAGE 102, BELOW

A circa-1900 photograph shows Seward's furnished room, which included family photographs, comfortable chairs, engravings, and his personal desk.

PAGE 103

A curved stairway in Seward's bedroom is connected to his personal valet's room above it.

BEDROOMS

LEFT

A detail of the decorative mantel pillar in Lila and Seward's daughter Frederica's bedroom, now called the Rose Room. The room went through a restoration in 1986–87. Inn guests staying in the room can enjoy many of the original furnishings and the bathroom retains its period fixtures and charm.

BELOW

A circa-1900 photograph of Frederica's bedroom shows the informal and personal style in which the family bedrooms were designed. They were often filled with family mementos and portraits, comfortable chairs and divans, and decorative fabrics and wallpapers popular at the time. In the right foreground, Frederica's grand piano is covered with an embroidered cloth.

OPPOSITE

Many of the guest bedrooms were decorated in various styles ranging from Colonial and Dutch to French Empire; they remain virtually the same today. The furnishings, wallpapers, carpets, and woodwork reflect the theme of each room's name. The Webbs traditionally reserved the Empire Room (seen here) for special guests.

BEDROOMS

ABOVE, LEFT, AND OPPOSITE
The Louis XVI Room is one of the most elegant bedrooms in the house and today retains the characteristic charm from the time when it was designed. Like the Empire Room, it was reserved for special guests—visiting politicians or social luminaries. Soft, blue-green, gray, and white hues, Rococo-carved furniture, and gilded bronze light fixtures characterize this style. The wallpaper is a reproduction of the original pattern, which, by mid-twentieth century, had been badly damaged. Copies of oil paintings of European nobility, such as the portrait over the bed of the infanta María Theresa of Spain (who married Louis XIV) by the Spanish painter Diego Velázquez, lend a regal air to the room.

BEDROOMS

LEFT AND OPPOSITE
The Dutch Room, at the top of the stairs above the Game Room, was among the guest rooms reserved for single guests. The original decoration included deep-brown wallpaper, dark stained woodwork, and marquetry furniture, which was in keeping with the spirit of seventeenth-century Dutch interiors. During the restoration, the beautiful Dutch tiles were preserved and the room was lightened up with pale painted walls and white woodwork.

BELOW LEFT
Several of the private bathrooms retain original marble sinks, nickel faucets and wall sconces, and deep, iron claw-foot bathtubs.

PAGES 110—111
In October, at the end of the Inn's season, the entire house is prepared for winter. Furniture and artwork are shrouded in sheets of white cotton, curtains are drawn, and doors are closed. Windows and doors are boarded up from the outside to protect the house from the cold winds blowing off Lake Champlain. The house sleeps in darkness until April, when the process is reversed and the house is again open to guests.

PAGES 112—113
Shelburne House closes for the winter—its window shades are drawn and its doors boarded over until springtime.

FORMAL GARDENS

The celebrated importance of Shelburne Farms' Formal Gardens, the sheer beauty of their design, and their unparalleled, stunning site are critical to garden history. The gardens are among the most beautiful historic country gardens in America. Their strong visual and social components are one of the many factors that contributed to the property's designation as a National Historic Landmark.

When it came to designing Shelburne's extensive landscape, the Webbs hired Frederick Law Olmsted to create a comprehensive plan; however, no professional designer is credited for the Formal Gardens and original plans have yet to be discovered. Lila Webb was a well-traveled, well-read, creative individual who had a keen interest in gardening and garden design. She mentions the development of her gardens in her personal correspondence with family and friends and in her journals. Many agree that the design is chiefly her creative expression.

In the 1980s, staff and volunteers who were working to revive the gardens began researching the evolution of Lila's garden design in order to create a new planting scheme for contemporary times. The brick walls were crumbling, steps had disappeared, and architectural elements, such as the two pergolas, were gone. Given the skeletal structure and layout of the gardens, they decided to adopt a Gertrude Jekyll–style garden and plantings to guide the next phase of its development.

Jekyll (1843–1932) was a highly influential English gardener and garden-book writer, who, with architect Sir Edwin Landseer Lutyens (1869–1944), transformed the approach to country-house gardening in England at the

PAGE 114

Today, the Formal Gardens are an expression of
Lila Webb's original design and vision.

BELOW

The circa-mid-1920s photograph taken by James
Watson Webb clearly illustrates the second of
Lila Webb's major garden designs, an Italianate
plan consisting of multileveled terraces and garden
"rooms." In the distance, the original north pergola
can be seen. Today, the north pergola is one of the
last remaining structures to be reinstated as part of
the decades-long restoration.

OPPOSITE

After Lila's death in 1936, the gardens slowly
declined. The garden walls deteriorated, and some
flowers and plants became overgrown while others
died. Over the past four decades, the original, brick
retaining walls and steps leading to and from the
terraced garden "rooms" were restored or removed
and rebuilt, following the conceptual plan that Lila
Webb had composed many decades earlier. Opti-
mum soil conditions and hardy plant materials were
also reestablished. Lila continually experimented
with and altered planting schemes. Today, the gardens are reinterpreted and planted in the spirit of
Gertrude Jekyll, the turn-of-the-twentieth-century
garden designer and garden-book writer who advocated movement through color and an informal mix
of perennial and annual flowers in a formal, struc-
tured setting.

turn of the twentieth century. She was a master of creating "drifts" of
harmonious, blended color and visual movement with the informal use of
perennials and annuals in the context of a formal garden structure, most
notably in the long borders of grand allées.

Although there were several Gertrude Jekyll garden books in Lila's personal library, no evidence was found that Lila ever tried Jekyll's approach to
color design in her own garden. However, Lila's experimentation did reveal
a strong influence of informal English garden traditions. She said of a visit
to England in 1913, "Some of the cottage gardens in Oxford I found very
beautiful and had two delightful days there."[8] In light of Lila's interests and
in recognizing that plantings continue to change and evolve in a thriving
garden, it seemed appropriate to everyone involved with the gardens' revival
to move forward with the goal of enhancing Lila's founding vision by drawing on the inspiration of Jekyll's ideas.

The current Formal Gardens are the result of a substantial restoration project begun in 1984 with the intention of reinterpreting the original
features of their overall structure, building materials, style, and plantings.
Through research and careful attention to details that appear in period
photographs, the essence of Lila's garden design has been revived and the
reinterpretation continues. The restoration will carry on until the majority
of the original structural and architectural features are completed.

The structural elements are from the second stage of Lila's design, completed around 1915. In the late 1890s, she had first introduced a large French
parterre-style garden, consisting of a series of geometric shapes that were

OPPOSITE

The handsome heraldic lion is one of a pair of sculptures that is the focal point on the steps between the second and third terraces. These symbols of wealth and taste of the period linked the riches of classical antiquity to the present, and have been part of the garden since its inception. Statuary from Greek and Roman mythology, antique urns, massive garden pots containing box or lemon trees, and substantial benches for comfortable seating are objects common in Italianate gardens of the era.

filled with plantings. "Bay trees and pyramidal boxwoods that surrounded the beds were dug up every winter and placed in the greenhouses."[9] "From about 1905 to 1915, Lila gathered ideas for further garden expansions and alterations during travels in Italy, France, Spain, England, and the western United States."[10] "She also drew influence from contemporary publications purchased for her extensive library, including Charles Platt's *Italianate Gardens* (1894), Edith Wharton's *Italian Villas and their Gardens* (1904), and Gertrude Jekyll's *Wall & Water Gardens* (1901)."[11] Lila's garden design is Italianate in style—a distinct nineteenth-century chapter in architecture and design that was inspired by classical antiquity and aesthetics. It became popular in America and was used for many civic buildings and private residences, as well as in garden design.

Formal gardens of the period were glorious places for relaxation, social intercourse, and the enjoyment of nature as much as they were symbols of wealth and taste. At Shelburne House, five distinct levels consisting of several garden "rooms" are delineated by low brick retaining walls and stone-capped balustrades, linked by stone steps. The gardens were at one time connected to the house by a terraced walkway from the north porch. One can imagine that the Webb family and their guests would, after breakfast or dinner, leave the dining room or terrace for a stroll through the gardens. The walkway would have been an inviting and easy transition from inside the house to the gardens' outdoor rooms.

Today, the final level in the gardens is the result of a challenging and impressive restabilization of the shoreline to reinstate land at the farthest point of the gardens that had been severely eroded and lost to the lake. On the garden side, a lily pool with a fountain head gently trickling water, bordered by Siberian iris, is echoed by a larger semicircular lawn and balustrade that reaches out high above the lake, offering stunning views in three directions of the vast Lake Champlain and the Adirondack Mountains across the water. Originally, large bay trees in striking pots were placed near the balustrade, providing decorative rhythm and a created sense of depth between the transitional space of land and lake.

The entire garden restoration is the splendid result of contributions and the work of consultants and volunteers who are passionate about Shelburne Farms and its gardens and eager to see the former grandeur of the place sensitively and appropriately reconstructed and shared with the public. The gardens are cared for throughout the year by building and maintaining good soil quality, planting new plants in the spring, cutting back plants in the fall, and tending and weeding the beds every week of the season.

Judging from period photographs over a few decades, Lila Webb experimented with many plantings, often a mix of annual plants and perennials—some could not survive the cold Vermont winters and would have been moved into the greenhouses. Several of Lila's flower choices remain in the garden today: peonies, delphinium, hollyhocks, iris, monkshood, yarrow, poppies, roses, hydrangea, and lots more. With the determination to make the gardens more sustainable, a hardy approach is in place today. Perennial plants that do well in Vermont's harsh winters are primary components to the overall planting scheme and a few annual plants are integrated to offer significant color and balance.

BELOW
The circa-1937 photograph taken by James Watson Webb Jr. shows the north pergola and reflecting pool.

OPPOSITE
Siberian iris were replanted and today surround the lower reflecting pool just as they did over one hundred years ago.

The gardens bloom from mid-May through October in an evolution of color and overall effect. From one end of the grand allée to the other, cool blues and whites at one end shift to warm yellows and vibrant reds in the middle and finally transition to pinks and cool blues at the other end. Masses of blooming plants assume a leading role for a time, such as the 'Queen Victoria' peonies in June, Asiatic lilies in July, sunflowers in August, and asters in September. The gardens are a colorful oasis that provide calmness to those who walk through them and take the time to absorb their serenity. Strolling from one level to another and from one garden room to another, the visual displays and scents emanating from the flowering plants, all under the umbrella of a majestic setting, are intoxicating.

Shelburne Farms' Formal Gardens have evolved over one hundred and more years. Today, guests at the farm and many others, including diners at the Inn, enjoy their splendor and effects. In the early evening, some of the restaurant's chefs appear in the gardens in their white cotton jackets to pick herbs and edible flowers. A fine selection of culinary plants such as mint, thyme, nasturtiums, sage, anise hyssop, and basil have been beautifully integrated into some of the gardens' beds, making it convenient for the cooks to use in preparing dishes, as finishing touches on plates, or as flavors in drinks.

The gardens provide the framework for pleasure, respite, and education. The historic site is an invaluable, thriving resource for garden scholars and an inspiration to home gardeners. Visitors on guided tours can learn about Shelburne House and its Formal Gardens. Of particular interest

BELOW, LEFT
Anemone canadensis is a perennial native to North America.

BELOW, RIGHT
Peony 'Festiva Maxima.'

OPPOSITE
Based on Lila's journals and plant lists, many of the perennial and annual plantings cultivated today are those that she enjoyed; however, only the 'Queen Victoria' peony stock is considered original.

PAGES 124–133
The multiple levels of the Formal Gardens are suggestive of similar-style, nineteenth-century gardens at Italian villas, where decisive architectural structure is predominant. The stone balustrades, ornamental statues, and water garden are closely aligned with Italianate-style features of the period. The descent from level to level culminates in a recently restored, magnificent, semicircular room that reaches out to Lake Champlain, offering stunning views of the lake and Adirondack Mountains across the water.

to visitors is knowing which plants are original to the garden. "Only the peonies are original stock from Lila's gardens. They have survived—and thrived—here for many decades."[12]

Just as Shelburne House is "put to bed" for the winter, the gardens undergo a similar process. By late October, the gardens' beds are cut back and become bare; only the physical structures remain. The gardens lie still throughout the frozen winter, until spring arrives and they awake again.

LEFT
Floribunda 'Iceberg' is one of the many winter-hardy roses in the rose garden.

BELOW, LEFT
Colorful annuals, such as zinnia, fill in the perennial plantings.

BELOW, RIGHT
The New England 'Purple Dome' aster blooms in September.

OPPOSITE
In July, the long borders are a brilliant display of color and texture that showcase perennials such as *Echinacea purpura* (commonly know as 'Purple Cone Flower').

PAGES 136–137
The final level in the gardens is the result of a remarkable restabilization of the shoreline to reinstate land at the farthest point of the gardens, which had been severely eroded and lost to the lake. Today, the reconstructed balustrade extends above the lake and offers stunning views.

LEFT

The water-holding vessel in the oval-shaped day-lily garden is original to the Formal Gardens. Today, the oval garden is located on the former site of the reflecting pool (see p. 120); this is one of the few garden structures to be reinstated.

BELOW

Drifts of texture and color are a nod to the Gertrude Jekyll–style gardens prevalent during Lila Webb's era.

OPPOSITE

The tree-form hydrangea 'Tardiva,' sunflower 'Summersonne,' and salvia 'Blue Hill' are among the many bold displays during July and August.

PAGES 140–143

In September, the gardens transition to magnificent displays of False Chamomile 'Snowbank' and a variety of dahlias.

PAGES 144–145

In October, the plants are cut back, offering uninterrupted views of the Formal Gardens' architectural components.

LEFT

From the Formal Gardens, the snow-covered pathway, bordered by juniper bushes, leads visitors on an informal, meandering trail through woodlands, populated by statuary, introduced by one of Lila's descendants.

BELOW

The 1937 photograph by James Watson Webb Jr. shows the mixed border leading to the south pergola, lightly covered with vines. Lila's approach to garden design included grass-covered pathways that led garden visitors to discover and delight in the movement and color created by "drifts" of hardy perennials and sweet-smelling annuals.

OPPOSITE

In winter, the Formal Gardens are bare and lie still until spring, when the gardens come alive again. Many of the gardens' architectural features had fallen into ruin by the mid-twentieth century. The south pergola was dismantled following a hurricane in 1953 and the parts were stored away in the Coach Barn attic. Based on period photographs, the pergola recently underwent restoration. Made of wood, the pieces were carefully repaired and the structure was reconstructed in its former location in 2015. The pergola provides an open wall-like framework at the southern end of the third level of garden terraces. It is also an intimate space for respite and socializing that has views of the opposite borders.

MAJOR BARNS

Three outstanding barns—the Farm Barn, Breeding Barn, and Coach Barn—are among the most distinguished structures at Shelburne Farms designed by Robert H. Robertson. At the time, the New York City architect was known for his tall skyscrapers, such as Park Row, the highest building in New York City in 1899. As pioneering as his Manhattan architecture was, his work in Shelburne, Vermont, became his magnum opus. "Shelburne Farms represented the most extensive architectural commission of Robertson's career. Between 1886 and 1905, he designed approximately thirty-six buildings and structures for Shelburne Farms in a combination of the Shingle and Queen Anne styles popular at the time."[13] Fifteen of these structures still stand, including the three major barns and Shelburne House. Three of the original eleven employee "tenant cottages" remain on the property. One serves as the Welcome Center, another as a guest cottage, located behind the Breeding Barn, and a third as staff lodging. Many of Robertson's buildings did not stand the test of time or use, such as a shepherd's cottage, a piggery, and a few minor barns. The Old Dairy Barn, located across from the Breeding Barn, was struck by lightning and burned to the ground in 2016. The structures were built in the same Shingle and Queen Anne styles but were not as grand in scale as the major barns.

The magnitude of Robertson's major architectural commission was of a scale that Vermont had not previously witnessed and certainly unlike the linear "connected farm" style that was common in nineteenth-century New England. Connected farms are one continuous structure of four or more linked buildings: the main house (living quarters), kitchen (utility), back house (for carriages and harnesses), and barn (livestock and feed storage). This type of farm dotted the Vermont landscape, and excellent examples exist today. The people who built these farm dwellings lived off the land—managing crops, growing food, raising livestock—practicing what we call today "self-sufficiency." Robertson did not design the Webbs' farm in the Vermont vernacular. However, the devotion to farming the land and country life was not dissimilar between the Webbs and their neighbors.

PAGES 148 AND 150–151
The magnificent Farm Barn looks much the same today as when it was was completed in 1890.

BELOW
The barn's massive scale alone surpassed any structure in Vermont at the time. As shown in its heyday in a circa-1900 photograph, the majestic combination of landscape and barn design was stunning. Due to a major restoration in the early 1990s, the Farm Barn today looks much as it did well over one hundred years ago.

OPPOSITE
The colossal towers located at the ends of the Farm Barn's two wings were possibly inspired by French châteaux. This is an unlikely site to come upon in rural Vermont—it feels like something out of a fairy tale.

PAGES 154–155
The Farm Barn's impressive front facade is composed of stone, shingle, and half-timbering. The sensitively composed arrangement of arched doorways and the variety of window shapes creates a decorative rhythm that was unprecedented in Vermont vernacular architecture of the late nineteenth century. Today, the Farm Barn houses the nonprofit organization's administrative offices, cheesemaking facilities, a bakery, and furniture workshop. Most visibly, it is the center of the Farms' education programs, including several indoor classrooms as well as the popular children's farmyard.

Robert H. Robertson began his major architectural commission for Lila and Seward Webb with the design of two buildings—their private residence and a barn, known as the Farm Barn. The barn was designed in 1886 and completed in 1890. It was intended as the epicenter of the "model" farm. The requirements were practical: to provide enough space for sheltering working animals and storage for hay and grains to feed the farm's animals, as well as space for offices, workshops, and machinery.

The Farm Barn was also a symbol of grandeur, wealth, and style. This functional farm structure's impressive design was unlike anything built in Vermont. Unlike the traditional post-and-beam wooden structures prevalent across vernacular Vermont, the five-story Farm Barn consists of stone, shingles, and half-timbering. Its unique layout wraps around a nearly two-acre open courtyard. Its stately character is reminiscent of fairy-tale castles and grand country estates in Europe, such as the Château de Bussy-Rabutin in Burgundy, France, which has a similar open courtyard around which a large main building is featured and two parallel side ells end with cone-roofed turrets.

For two decades, the Farm Barn was a center of agricultural activities and it was Vermont's largest and most impressive farm building, providing unprecedented, innovative spaces in one complex for numerous horse stables, work mules, farm equipment, and hay and grain storage. But as time went on and finances became more of a concern, major cutbacks in staff

BELOW
The circa-1900 photograph reveals the nearly two-acre open courtyard around which the Farm Barn and its two wings are built. The barn was the center of activity on the farm, sheltering animals and providing storage for hay and grains. It was also where the farm manager's office and farmers' workshops were located.

OPPOSITE
The magnificent facade of the Farm Barn highlights its turn-of-the-twentieth-century design and materiality: stone, shingle, and half-timbering siding, mullion windows, and a copper roof. From high above its five-story structure, the tower's old clock—still wound the old-fashioned way—strikes each day on the hour, letting everyone around the barn know the time.

and farming activities took place. The building, like many other buildings on the property, had witnessed hard times and began to slip into decline. In 1972, the newly formed Shelburne Farms nonprofit organization moved into part of the barn and created the strategy for today's Shelburne Farms. From 1990 to 1993, the barn underwent a major renovation to become an education center.

Today, the great barn is the center of Shelburne Farms' education planning and many of its programs and activities that take place in the classrooms of the McClure Center for School Programs. The barn is also home to the children's farmyard. Cheesemaking has a significant presence in the barn, offering visitors a view of the steps to making Shelburne Farms' world-famous Cheddar. A few program partners are also located there, including an organic bakery and a furniture workshop.

Shelburne Farms' education team conducts workshops and offers accredited courses. They also provide outreach to schools, and work with educators on developing curriculum based around the unique resources of their own communities. Looking to foster change by inspiring children to learn more about the food they eat, one important initiative focuses on food education to encourage improvement in the quality of school food systems by inspiring students to make healthier choices. An essential aspect of Shelburne Farms' education mission is to strengthen, renew, and rebuild relationships among people of all ages, using nature and the land as the catalysts for learning. The property—land, forests, barns, and buildings—is indeed a living classroom.

PAGES 158–161
The children's farmyard is a living classroom where students learn about farm animals. Friendly chickens; kid, nanny, and billy goats; pigs and piglets; calves and cows; and lambs are an integral part of the Farm Barn and its education activities.

OPPOSITE
A Brown Swiss cow from the farm's herd contentedly rests on a clean, soft bed of sawdust before a milking demonstration at the children's farmyard.

Three-quarters of a mile from the Farm Barn is the enormous Shingle-style Breeding Barn, designed by Robert H. Robertson as another major component of Lila and Seward Webb's "model" farm. The barn's purpose was to shelter, showcase, and breed the Hackney horse. At 418 feet long and 107 feet wide, the barn was the showpiece among a number of barns built on the southern part of the property that were created for the horse-breeding enterprise. Known early on as the Ring Barn, it included an interior horse-exercise ring, 375 feet long and 85 feet wide, as well as sixty-five boxed stalls, harness rooms, workshops, hay storage lofts, and staff apartments. Unlike most barns in Vermont at this time, the Breeding Barn was state-of-the-art, and was even designed for electricity. The interior space was a marvel; not only was it uninterrupted by any supporting columns, but it was also illuminated by a series of "1,000 electric lights, which are arranged as to permit no shadow around the arena."[14]

Seward wanted to breed an ideal horse that was versatile and not unlike Vermont's famous Morgan horse: strong enough to pull a plow or carriage and elegant enough to ride in a saddle. The English Hackney possessed the qualities Seward was seeking to breed and make popular in Vermont and beyond. "The horse breeding operation was by far the most extensive component of the estate's stock farm. Seward intended Shelburne Farms to be one of the largest and most important horse farms in the country. The stud program attracted customers from across the United States and as far

BELOW
The circa-1900 photograph offers a view of the Breeding Barn in its heyday, during its first decade of use.

OPPOSITE
The massive Shingle-style Breeding Barn underwent a significant restoration in the 1990s.

PAGES 164–165
The Breeding Barn's front facade looks much the same as it did over one hundred years ago. To visitors who were used to seeing post-and-beam English-style barns that dotted the Vermont landscape, it was a "modern" marvel.

BELOW
When it was constructed in 1891, the Breeding Barn, known then as the Ring Barn, included a large horse exercise and training arena and sixty-five loose boxed stalls.

OPPOSITE
Today, the barn is largely used for farm purposes and storage, but the magnificent open interior comes alive in new ways when it is transformed for educational, agricultural, or cultural events.

away as Warsaw."[15] Seward's ambitious experiment to incorporate strength and beauty in one breed quickly yielded to a dawning technological era: the development of the internal combustion engine changed farmwork and transportation forever, causing his dream of the perfect country horse to dissolve. After a decade of work, the horse-breeding operation ceased activity.

Lila and Seward began to divide up the Shelburne Farms' property and gifted acreage to their children. They gave a significant portion of land, which included the Breeding Barn, to their eldest son, James Watson Webb. The property, known as "Southern Acres," was separated from Shelburne Farms in 1913. Over the next few decades, James Watson used the barn to shelter his own cattle, for feed storage, and for sporting activities such as indoor polo. In 1994, Shelburne Farms was able to reunite the Breeding Barn and the neighboring Dairy Barn as well as four hundred acres of glorious land surrounding them. Restoration of the barn began in 1996 by reinforcing its structure and replacing its two-acre roof with 88,000 pounds of copper roofing.

Entering the Breeding Barn feels like an agricultural version of a great cathedral; the vast space is beautiful and awe-inspiring. Today, while it undergoes continuing restoration, the barn is used for farm-related storage, but it is ultimately intended to become a great hall for educational and agricultural uses to bring educators and communities together under one inspiring roof.

BELOW

One of Seward Webb's elegant Hackney horses stands outside the main entrance to the Breeding Barn in a circa-1895 photograph.

OPPOSITE

The traverse side of the Breeding Barn, looking through the main entrance, provides a view to the allée of trees outside.

PAGES 170–171

View of the Breeding Barn's wooden ceiling and cupola with its intricate system of steel tie rods.

COACH BARN

The sophisticated Coach Barn was designed to accommodate the desires and reflect the lifestyle of an affluent family living on a country estate. Situated close to Shelburne House and a lake cove, the barn served as the family's transportation and pleasure-riding headquarters. Completed in 1901, the Coach Barn was the last major building Robertson designed for Shelburne Farms. Originally, horses were stabled in the barn's thirty-two stalls, immaculate tack was neatly organized in large, finely trimmed rooms with vertical tongue-and-groove woodwork, and over thirty carriages and sleighs offered the Webbs and their friends elegant options for travel. Groomsmen lived in apartments upstairs. "In 1905, the Coach Barn housed twenty-three horses: fourteen carriage horses, including a four-in-hand team; six saddle horses; a horse to pull the farm baggage wagon; and two ponies for the children."[16]

Beauty reigns through the design of the building's stately architecture and materials. The impressive redbrick building retains its original slate roof and an iron gate at its entryway. The barn possesses a splendid interior courtyard that is accessed through a Richardsonian-style brick arched gateway. Inside, protected from the winds sweeping across Lake Champlain by its four sides, the courtyard is both an interior and exterior chamber; the sky is its ceiling. From inside the courtyard, a look through the arched entrance provides a view of the lake in the distance.

BELOW
The circa-1900 photograph of the old Coach Barn's tack room illustrates the care and order taken to store the extensive collection of horse saddles and harnesses.

OPPOSITE
In 1902, just after the second Coach Barn was completed, horses, carriages, and riders passed through its magnificent arched entranceway to enter the courtyard, where riders dismounted and horses and carriages were taken into the first-floor washroom.

PAGES 174–175
The stately barn had seen many uses over the years, but today looks much the same way it did over a century ago. It is an inspiring place for community gatherings, educational conferences, art shows, and special events.

BELOW
The circa-1902 photograph shows the clean environment and loose box stalls in which the horses rested and slept when not in service or out in pasture.

OPPOSITE
Occasionally, coaching and horse clubs utilize the Coach Barn's stalls. During their stay, carriage drivers explore miles of extensive roads with expansive views of two mountain ranges and Lake Champlain.

Like the state-of-the-art Breeding Barn, the Coach Barn was wired for electricity and telegraph, making it easy for the Webbs to call from the house to the barn when they needed to make arrangements for travel, coaching, or riding. Inside, an innovative platform elevator enabled carriages and equipment to be easily moved from the first-floor washroom up to the second floor for storage. The head coachman's house, built next to the Coach Barn, is a scaled-back design that is similar in style to the impressive barn.

During the years of transition, the Coach Barn witnessed many uses beyond its primary one as a center for horse and riding activities. In the early part of the twentieth century, it stored the Webbs' automobiles and carriages. By mid-century the carriages were donated to the nearby Shelburne Museum, where they can be seen. In the 1950s and 1960s, the barn housed sheep, pigs, and cows. It was also the site for the farm's cattle auctions. In 1972, as plans were shaping up for Shelburne Farms to become an educational nonprofit organization with a focus on agriculture and the environment, the Coach Barn first served as the center for its school field trips and educator workshops. Today, the Coach Barn is a multipurpose building that provides inspiring classrooms and event spaces in a beautiful setting. It is also used for other nonprofit organization events, such as the Vermont Fresh Network's Annual Forum dinner, and the Vermont Cheesemakers Festival.

LEFT, OPPOSITE, AND PAGES 180–183
Several views of the exterior of the Coach Barn illustrate the character, style, and details of Robert H. Robertson's last major building design for Shelburne Farms.

BELOW
James Watson Webb on a Wagonette Break, driving a four-in-hand team, on the Shelburne Farms property, circa 1899.

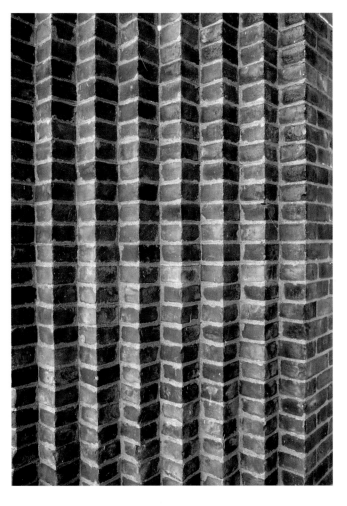

FARMING THE LAND

Shelburne Farms lies in the Champlain Valley, a vast stretch of land bordering Lake Champlain, a large, 490-square-mile, freshwater lake that borders New York and Vermont and stretches north to the Canadian province of Quebec. The property, like its neighbors on the Vermont side of the lake, possesses one of the longest growing seasons and some of the most fertile soil in the state. Europeans first settled in the region in the second half of the 1700s, clearing and farming the land for agricultural purposes. For centuries before their arrival, it was an important natural, forested hunting ground for the Abenaki, a Native American tribe and one of the Algonquian-speaking peoples of North America, who seasonally moved throughout New England and the Maritime provinces.

Vermont's natural resources became severely depleted in the early 1800s as a result of deforestation for timber sales and the clearing of the land to create pastures for the Merino sheep industry, a decades-long market for wool. The state had prospered from these flourishing industries but its natural landscape was destabilized in the process. The wool boom collapsed by the mid-nineteenth century. Not all Vermonters were part of the timber or sheep industries; many made their livelihoods from farming the land.

Dr. William Seward Webb was a member of the founding generation of the environmental movement. Like-minded individuals, such as George Perkins Marsh (1801–1882), one of the founders of the environmental movement and author of *Man and Nature* (1864), and Frederick Billings (1823–1890), who put Marsh's conservationist philosophies into practice at his Woodstock, Vermont, estate, wished to restore the natural environment

PAGE 184
At the Vegetable Garden, known as the "market garden," seeds are started in the greenhouses to give them a strong, healthy life. In May, when they are large and strong enough, they are planted outside in the field gardens, where they continue to flourish in the open air and sunshine. In 1985, Shelburne Farms was one of the first Vermont vegetable gardens to be certified organic.

BELOW

During the nineteenth century, the farms' staff did most of the farmwork by hand with hand tools. The Webbs employed seasonal and year-round staff, some of whom gathered with the farm manager (seated in the carriage) in this 1893 photograph.

OPPOSITE

Today, close to six hundred acres of the farms' total acreage is devoted to hay fields. Hay is composed of grass, clover, and other herbaceous plants. Hay is cut in spring and summer, after which it is baled as silage or dry hay for animal consumption during the winter months.

by returning it to its proper ecological balance. During this period, new science in farming was part of that interest. Seward was intent on creating a model farm in Vermont; one that he hoped would instruct and inspire not only local farmers, but also agriculturalists beyond the region and across the country. Seward and Lila achieved a notable degree of success in this ambitious venture. During its heyday, "Shelburne Farms was known as one of the foremost farms in the country."[17] Historian Erica Huyler Donnis explains, "At the turn of the twentieth century, Shelburne Farms was devoted to experimenting with the latest agricultural technology and scientific practices. In ideal terms, model farms operated under a 'trickle-down' theory: those who could afford to develop and test new approaches would disseminate their results to a broader audience through correspondence with professionals in the field, through the press, and through local word of mouth. By doing so, they would eventually assist in improving production and increasing profits for everyday farmers. Meanwhile, model farm owners would provide their own tables with choice farm products."[18]

In the early-nineteenth century, with Vermont's population growth, new farms were established. On the site of the present Shelburne Farms, there were several small subsistence farms. These farmers produced enough to sustain their families and livestock. Due to the fertile soil, mild climate, quality of the pastures, and the type of crops they grew, many became prosperous by selling products—such as apples, dairy, and eggs—to neighboring Vermont towns. This community of farms changed when Lila and Seward Webb set their sights on building an idyllic, pastoral estate, and

OPPOSITE
Most of the farms' cows are bred to calve in the spring from March to June and some are bred to calve in the autumn. Heifer calves are raised on colostrum from their mother for their first three feedings, then on their mother's milk. They are gradually weaned to water and begin eating hay. At sixty days they are completely weaned. In their second summer, heifers go out to pasture. They have their first calf at two years of age and then join the milking herd.

PAGES 190—191
Once weaned from their mothers, young cattle are allowed to roam in large pastures. The meat from beef animals is used at Shelburne Farms' restaurant, farm cart, and store. Particular superior dairy bulls are raised as purebred breeding stock and some are sold to other farms. In 2006, Shelburne Farms was the first farm in Vermont to be awarded "Certified Humane Farm," for the humane treatment of its livestock.

subsequently purchased much of the surrounding farmlands. Donnis explains, "The Webbs' newly established estate of Shelburne Farms united more than thirty individual farms, replacing one community with a different one. The Webbs came from quite a different background and brought a new perspective and way of life to the area. However, they ultimately shared a common goal with the families from whom they purchased their property: to farm the land."[19] By the 1890s, the Webbs acquired land and farms of various sizes in Shelburne and created a contiguous property of close to 3,800 acres.

Lila and Seward created orchards and planted apple trees on the property that "produced as many as 5,000 barrels of apples, including Spies, Greenings, and Baldwins. Barrels were regularly sent to the Webbs' residences and to family, friends, and employees as gifts."[20] They built magnificent glass greenhouses and vegetable gardens for growing produce to feed themselves, staff, and their numerous houseguests. Flowers were cultivated to adorn their home. Hackney horses, Southdown sheep, pigs, Jersey dairy and beef cattle, chickens, and game birds were raised.

In the 1940s, Lila and Seward's grandson, Derick Webb (1913–1984), took over the management of the farm and focused on dairy as a way to make the farm financially viable. He experimented with a variety of cow breeds and raised cattle, which he sold each year at an auction on the property. In 1952, he built a new dairy barn on the site of the golf links that is now home to the purebred herd of Brown Swiss cows he had established.

The new environmental awareness that emerged in the 1960s and 1970s inspired changing farming practices at Shelburne Farms. The back-to-the-land movement was prevalent in pockets of rural areas in the United States from coast to coast and it took hold at Shelburne Farms with some of Lila and Seward's descendants. The movement's call to urbanites to become farmers was to take small agricultural spaces and grow food on the land on a small scale to feed the farmers themselves, their families, or nearby communities. Strong influences were books such as *A Sand County Almanac* (1948) by ecologist and environmentalist Aldo Leopold, who advocated a "land ethic," or the ethical, responsible relationship in which people should regard the land, animals, and plants that grow upon it, and *Living the Good Life* (1954) by Vermonters Helen and Scott Nearing, who advocated self-sufficiency, growing one's own food, and maintaining a simple lifestyle. By the 1980s, the farm switched to grass-based livestock farming to improve environmental health and economic viability. The farm also began to raise and grow more and more of its own food.

The adopted land ethic embraces the well-being of wildlife. Shelburne Farms' woodlands and landscape plantings, including islands of trees, provide protection from strong winds and shady places for the herd, as well as habitat for many species of birds and animals that are vital and beneficial to the the entire local ecosystem. The farm currently manages a significant portion of its hay land to provide breeding habitat for endangered field-nesting songbirds.

Today, in early spring, Shelburne Farms' greenhouses, animal barns, and maple sugarbush are about promise and the potential of growth in the coming year. In the barns, young stock are born to Brown Swiss cows and

OPPOSITE

Two newborn goats make their home at the children's farmyard at the Farm Barn where they become an integral part of the education programs that teach children, families, and educators about the care and raising of livestock.

lambing begins; this is the time when the ewes give birth. The heartwarming sounds of bleating lambs and "moos" of young stock are mingled with the earthy smells of straw, hay, and manure. In Vermont, freezing temperatures continue outside, but inside the warm, humid greenhouses seeds are planted, and soon thousands of seeds sprout into tiny green plants. Calm prevails, occasionally broken by the sound of a soft mist from a garden hose or the honking calls of Canada geese flying above, returning home to their nesting grounds.

The newborn animals and tender seedlings emerge at a time of year when Vermont is in transition. With one leg in the last weeks of winter and the other planted in early spring, the vegetable gardeners and livestock and dairy farmers prepare for the growing season. As spring unfolds into summer, the days become increasingly warmer and longer, the landscape turns many shades of green, and tender young things grow stronger and larger.

Education runs deep at Shelburne Farms. It began with Lila and Seward's interest in learning more about effective agricultural practices, acting on that knowledge, and sharing that experience. Their goal in creating a subsistent farm was to effect positive change for the improvement of the land and farming practices that would ultimately help farmers and others to create healthy agricultural products and livestock. At that time, visitors to the farm benefited from firsthand observation. Outside Shelburne, farm journals, magazines, and newspaper articles became the vehicles for conveying the progressive work at Shelburne Farms.

One hundred and thirty years later, the nonprofit organization that is now Shelburne Farms has benefited from several decades of national and international environmental research and agricultural practice, which in turn, it offers to a widening audience around the country, eager to learn about land stewardship. This working farm uses its practices and the food it produces to educate people of all ages about sustainable agriculture. Shelburne Farms encourages people to put that learning into practice on personal, local, and regional levels, believing that when individuals can effect positive environmental changes in communities, the world can become a healthier and more beautiful place.

Shelburne Farms follows organic and sustainable farming practices in each of its food endeavors—the vegetable garden, dairy farm, lamb and beef production, raising free-range chickens for fresh eggs, and maple sugaring. The farm's holistic approach to raising and growing ingredients results in food that is wholesome and tastes delicious.

Important to Shelburne Farms' mission is that its developmental processes do not deplete natural resources or harm the environment. Shelburne Farms works to build and maintain a balanced ecology of its soils through its farm, gardens, and woodlands. An impressive sustainable local food system has been achieved. The food it raises and grows honors the land it comes from. Following the "land ethic" philosophy laid out by Aldo Leopold decades earlier, by integrating its agricultural goals with hands-on educational and cultural experiences, Shelburne Farms promotes a healthful future for land, animals, plants, and people, while underscoring the important connections between them.

THE DAIRY FARM

The Dairy Farm is integral to Shelburne Farms' intensive grass-based farming system story. At its heart is the magnificent, prized herd of 110 purebred Brown Swiss cows, acclaimed to be the oldest continually operated Brown Swiss herd in the United States. Brown Swiss cows originated in the Alps in Switzerland and were first introduced to North America in 1869. This breed is known for the high fat and protein content in its milk, which is the perfect ingredient for making Cheddar cheese. In the 1950s, farm manager Derick Webb, grandson of Lila and Seward, refocused the farm and its activities, one of which was to raise Brown Swiss cows for milk. He chose the breed for its hardiness to live in Vermont's cold winter climate, grazing capacity, milk quality, long life, and gentle temperament. At first, the dairy farm sold raw milk to sources off the farm in order to generate income; decades later it shifted its production to using all its herd's milk to make Cheddar cheese on the farm.

In "intensive" grass-based farming, rotational grazing is critical to the balance of the whole system. Cows forage in one- or two-acre contained areas of pasture for twelve to twenty-four hours; then they are moved to another fresh pasture. The previous pasture is allowed to rest for two to five weeks so that the plants can recover and grow. Manure droppings from the cows return essential nutrients to the soil. By moving each day to new pastures, the herd is constantly feeding on a fresh, green "salad" of plants. The system reduces adverse environmental impact; there is less need for machinery and fuel to manage the growth and cutting of pastureland, and soil erosion and runoff is vastly reduced by not plowing fields. The cows are an integral and natural part of the process.

Brown Swiss cows are a friendly, easygoing breed. Heifers—young female cows that have not borne a calf—are gradually weaned from feeding on their mothers' milk and then introduced to eating hay. In their second summer, they transition to pasture feeding. They give birth to their first calf at two years, and join the herd of milking cows. Milking cows are brought in from pasture and milked twice a day, once in the morning at 4:30 a.m. and then in afternoon at 3:30 p.m. Each cow produces an average of fifty-five pounds of milk a day, the equivalent of six to seven gallons.

Shelburne Farms was the first dairy in Vermont to be formally recognized as a "Certified Humane Farm," a designation it received in 2006 for its humane treatment of livestock. The average cow has at least three lactations and can provide milk for five to ten years. Brown Swiss cows can live twelve to sixteen years, a bit longer than the national average for dairy cows. One cow in the herd, "Shelburne Del 514," lived to be seventeen. Some of the farm's livestock, however, is bred and raised annually for meat. The dairy farm is also responsible for cultivating a flock of crossbred sheep; approximately one hundred lambs are processed for meat each year to be used at the Inn's restaurant. It also raises approximately twenty cows for beef and in some years has raised pigs for pork. The farm's manager believes that "it is important to treat the animals with respect and dignity. It starts the day the animal is born and continues each day by treating the animal kindly. They bond with us and look to us for their care and well-being."

OPPOSITE

At the heart of the farm, there are over one hundred purebred Brown Swiss cows, acclaimed for being the oldest continually operated Brown Swiss herd in the United States. The Brown Swiss breed is known for its immense size, large furry ears, and resistance to heat and cold. The high fat and protein content in their milk is the perfect ingredient for making Cheddar cheese. To provide the best nutrition for the cows, the dairy farm practices rotational grazing. The cows roam free in two-acre contained pastures for a day and graze on a "salad" of pasture plants. They are moved to another contained, fresh pasture for another day of grazing. The former pasture is given two to five weeks rest to allow plants to grow back. The vast amount of pastureland allows the rotational process to continue through the growing season and provides the cows with the highest quality ingredients each day. These healthy, well-nourished cows produce a milk with a ratio of protein to fat that is ideal for cheesemaking. Their milk is used to produce Shelburne Farms' famous farmstead Cheddar cheese.

From the outset, the Webbs' gardeners grew and supplied vegetables and fruits for the family's tables and pantries at Shelburne House, where entertaining was often at a grand scale. They also sent fresh produce, milk, and flowers by train from the Shelburne train depot to family members in New York City.

Shelburne Farms' original, magnificent glass greenhouses are no longer standing, but during their heyday they also produced flowers including gardenias, palm trees, and many exotic plants to enhance Shelburne House with aromatic scents and colorful displays. The visual grandeur and design of the turn-of-the-century vegetable garden has been transformed to a different, but an equally impressive one for the twenty-first century. Today, on the same site, several contemporary hoop greenhouses and field gardens operate as a seven-acre garden to produce beautiful, healthy vegetables, herbs, fruits, and flowers, most of which make their way to the dining tables at the Inn at Shelburne Farms and as farm shares, provided to over sixty staff members each week.

The highly regarded Vegetable Garden, known as the "market garden," operates with the careful management of land, soil, and natural resources. In fact, Shelburne Farms was one of the first vegetable gardens in Vermont to be certified organic, in 1985. Third-party regulatory certification, such as Vermont's Northeast Organic Farming Association (NOFA), assures consumers of the honest quality of the food the farm produces. One of Shelburne Farms' top priorities is to sustain healthy, fertile soil conditions for its gardens through organic growing practices. Soil is important to the health and nature of plant life, and the produce from plants become the ingredients that people consume. "Clean" ingredients are those that have been nourished through natural systems that include soil, nutrients, sun, and water, as well as scientific knowledge and a lot of tender care.

The garden manager describes vegetable farming with the adage, "Farmers raise or grow food to feed people." The food farmers provide is essentially raw ingredients that are prepared or cooked and then served and consumed. The taste of food has everything to do with the growing conditions of the raw ingredients. Passionate gardeners agree that the quality of the ingredients they grow eventually comes down to the land and soil—the chemistry and nutrients that ultimately affect taste. Some chefs yearn to impart the terroir, a French term that describes particular epicurean subtleties in crops that are developed as a result of the specific habitat in which they are grown.

The Vegetable Garden's activities provide clear connections between the land, produce, and people. Its manager has developed a demonstrative "classroom" designed to illustrate sustainable food systems, which is open to visitors of all ages, whether they are local people who are walking the property's trails and stop to take a look at what is growing that day, young summer campers spending a week at Shelburne Farms to help harvest and cook their own food for the first time, or college students who are surveying holistic food systems in the Northeast. The Vegetable Garden encourages inquiry and allows dialogue to happen easily. This open-space classroom

OPPOSITE
The Vegetable Garden was in 1985 one of Vermont's first gardens to be certified organic, an official third-party recognition that assures consumers of the honest methods by which the produce is grown. By midsummer, the garden supplies nearly all of the fruits and vegetables that are prepared and served at the Inn's restaurant.

OPPOSITE

A fourteen-acre "sugarbush," composed of hundreds of maple trees, provides maple sap, which is collected in late winter to make pure maple syrup. The trees are "tapped" by drilling small holes in their trunks to collect the sap. Over two miles of plastic tubing are used to collect the sap that makes its way to the state-of-the-art sugarhouse, built in 2016, near the Vegetable Garden. A part of the sugarbush is located on the hill behind the Farm Barn, where the children's sugarhouse is the classroom for students and families who participate in the annual sap-to-syrup tradition.

for learning is not intimidating—it is diverse, well organized, clean, and aesthetically appealing. The Vegetable Garden is full of activity throughout the year, not just during the summer months. Engaging projects, such as improvements to the greenhouse design, pruning apple trees, or planting a new crop, are ongoing.

MAPLE SUGARING

Honoring one of Vermont's best known and revered traditions, Shelburne Farms operates a "sugarbush," a fourteen-acre stand of maple trees from which sap is collected to make pure maple syrup. Maple sap was first collected and made into syrup by the Native American Abenaki well before Vermont was established in 1761. European settlers learned from them, and then refined their boiling technique. Today, developments in technology and equipment have improved and simplified the process.

A cold climate is necessary to the success and quality of making maple syrup. During the warm time of the year, maple trees store starch in their roots and trunks. The starch is converted to sugar that rises due to shifts in temperature from freezing to above freezing. Maple sugaring begins as early as late January and can end at the beginning of April, depending on the temperature. At Shelburne Farms, when sap "runs," it is collected from two and a half miles of plastic tubing "tapped" into the maple trees to make hundreds of gallons of syrup.

This special wild food is native to the Northeast and has made Vermont world-famous as the largest producer of maple syrup in the United States. Vermonters take great pride in the exceptional quality and taste of their pure maple syrup. North of Vermont, in the Canadian province of Quebec, making maple syrup is also an important industry. Quebec produces about three-quarters of the world's maple syrup. Maple syrup is often associated with breakfast—poured onto pancakes and French toast. The chefs at the Inn's restaurant also use it as an ingredient in salad dressings and in many dishes, such as a sweetener for its Maple Tarts with Candied Spruce Tips (see page 268). Shelburne Farms participates in the annual statewide "Vermont Maple Open House Weekend" that is held in March. Visitors are invited to participate in the sap-to-syrup process.

The Dairy Farm, Vegetable Garden, and Maple Sugaring operation are critical partners with Shelburne Farms' farm-to-table dining experiences. The unified food system provides many of the restaurant's primary ingredients on a seasonal basis—organic fruits, vegetables, herbs, and mushrooms; pasture-raised beef, veal, lamb, and pork; pastured eggs; Cheddar cheese; and maple syrup—supporting the economic vitality of the whole organization. Shelburne Farms sells its products on the property, by mail order, and through other outlets. Proceeds from sales are reinvested into educational programs to benefit children, families, and educators.

At Shelburne Farms, both experiencing such activities as cheesemaking and observing the Vegetable Garden's evolution throughout the spring and summer pave the way for learning firsthand. They are meant to be collaborative opportunities for all participants to learn from one another and to share those discoveries beyond this magnificent, vast property.

LEFT
Brown Swiss cows are noted for their gentle manner and good-natured temperament.

BELOW
In the Dairy Farm Barn's milking parlor, the cows move through an efficient system of gates. Twelve cows line up on one side of the milking pit and are cleaned and prepped for milking by the herdsman. As they are milked, twelve more cows file down the other side of the pit and are prepped. Once a cow from the first side has been milked, the milking machine swings over to the other side to milk another cow. After one row of cows has been milked, they walk out to pasture and a new group of cows takes their place. Milking cows are brought in from pasture and milked twice a day, once early in the morning at 4:30 a.m. and in the late afternoon at 3:30 p.m. Each cow produces an average of fifty-five pounds of milk a day, the equivalent of six to seven gallons.

OPPOSITE
During the cold winter months, when outdoor pasturing is not possible, after the cows are milked they walk into a large open-space barn and are provided a generous meal of silage. The space is filled with sunlight, and the cows are able to roam and relax.

LEFT

The cheesemaking facility is located in the Farm Barn. The food production system begins with cows grazing on the beautiful, healthy pasturelands and ends with the making of Shelburne Farms' legendary food product, farmstead Cheddar cheese.

BELOW, LEFT

Smoked Cheddar is the result of imbuing the cheese for six hours with the smoke from smoldering hickory wood.

BELOW, RIGHT

Cheddar is often used as an ingredient in cooking, such as in Smoked Cheddar and Maple Stout Soup (see recipe on page 250).

OPPOSITE

The clothbound Cheddar is aged in a cheese cave for over a year.

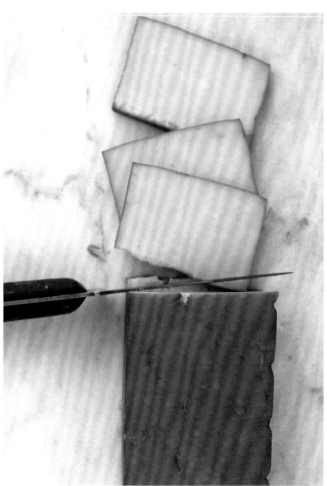

Lambing begins in late winter. Newborn lambs start their lives with their mothers in a clean, dry, hay-covered wooden barn near the Dairy Farm Barn. The barn in April is a beautiful sight, full of sunlight streaming in, like a cozy blanket, on the gentle little creatures. After a few weeks, the lambs and ewes move outside, where they graze freely in grassy pastures.

Shelburne Farms cultivates a flock of crossbred sheep: Tunis, Polypay, Dorset, and Leicester. The farm's mixed breed is noted for the quality of its meat. A small, purebred flock of Navajo-Churro sheep, a strong breed that originated from Spanish-raised sheep and refined by Native American nations in the American West centuries ago, also roam the property. They are part of a special micro program. The Navajo-Churro breed is renowned for its hardiness and adaptability to Vermont's long, cold winters as well as for its easygoing temperament. The flock was donated to Shelburne Farms years ago, and the herd's prized wool is annually sent back to the Navajo reservation, where traditional weavers use it to make wool rugs with sustainable wool.

Shelburne Farms' lambs' meat is tender and flavorful, and the wool is made into yarn. From the flock of cross-bred sheep, approximately one hundred lambs are raised annually to be processed for meat. Ninety lambs are used by the Inn's restaurant; the remainder is sold at Shelburne Farms' store.

Sheep are mild, skittish creatures, but despite their seemingly nervous disposition they are a beautiful presence on the farm's pastoral landscape and are an important part of its local, sustainable food-product system.

Inside the henhouse are several nesting boxes, lined with hay, where the hens lay eggs.

The farm's assistant woodlands manager oversees the maple sugaring operation as well as the cultivation of mushrooms, which was started in 2011 as part of a cooperative study with Cornell University and the University of Vermont to investigate the viability of growing mushrooms in Northeast woodlands. Logs are cut in February and inoculated with the spore of shitake mushrooms in early spring. Leftover wax from the cheesemaking process is used to seal the bore holes. The logs produce two "flushes" a year, in the spring and early summer, about six to eight weeks apart.

Three-hundred logs are first "shocked" by submerging them in a cold-water bath for one day. They are then stacked in a shady woodshed where they are protected from slugs and rain. Five days later, the "fruiting" begins and mushrooms emerge during the "flush," the short time when they grow. Each log produces about a half-pound of shitake mushrooms per flush, about one pound per year, adding up to approximately three-hundred pounds of mushrooms each season. Like all food ingredients that are grown at the Vegetable Garden, the mushrooms are delivered to the Inn's restaurant, where they are prepared and served in season.

The barnlike, portable henhouse on wheels moves around the property. It stops at a new location every few days to provide the flock with fresh feeding grounds. Chickens scratch the earth and forage for insects, grubs, and worms, and they eat small plants. The freedom they are afforded on the open land, combined with clean, sunny conditions, contributes to the health of each chicken and to the greater flock.

The magnificent glass greenhouses that appear in the circa-1900 photograph are long gone. Shown is the head gardener, formally dressed, while he prunes plants. Today's vegetable and flower growing continues at the same location on seven acres of agricultural land in a quiet spot on the property that is protected from the strong winds blowing in from Lake Champlain.

Several "hoop" greenhouses are located in the same area as the glass greenhouses were over a hundred years ago. Today, the greenhouses and "field" vegetable gardens are called the "market garden." The Vegetable Garden follows the basic principles of the organic food movement that revolutionized honest and healthy gardening practices in the 1970s. Lila and Seward's descendants were a part of the movement. They put principles into action and inspired others to do the same: establish a small farm to grow diversified products to sell directly to consumers in order to obtain a better price and establish a strong interaction between the consumer and producer. The Vegetable Garden's main consumer is Shelburne Farms' kitchen at the Inn. It supplies nearly all of the produce that is used for cooking meals at the restaurant, the farm cart at the Farm Barn, and special catered events at the Coach Barn and other locations around the property.

LEFT AND BELOW
The vegetable gardener oversees the production of mixed vegetables from seed to harvest to delivery. The growing season starts around late March when the first seeds are planted in the greenhouses and it continues throughout the summer and into October, yielding a vast array of vegetables, herbs, fruits, and flowers. Its clean, robust production on a small scale is an important model of organic farming and clearly illustrates the contemporary farm-to-plate movement at its best. The Vegetable Garden is a visible and active demonstration of the sustainable practices that Shelburne Farms seeks to inspire.

PAGES 216–217
The hoop greenhouses provide plants with warmth and protection.

COUNTERCLOCKWISE FROM LEFT:
The varied green colors and textures, such as mustard greens, spinach, mesclun, Swiss chard, basil, cabbage, and chervil, are extraordinary.

PAGES 220 and 221
The field gardens are planted with rows of salad greens, vegetables, and flowers in May, when the daily temperatures begin to stay above freezing.

COUNTERCLOCKWISE FROM LEFT:
Black raspberry, red currant, black currant, purple bells, pot marigold, 'Sweet William,' and foxgloves.

PAGE 224
Curly kale is planted in the field garden.

PAGE 225
Tomatoes ripen in the hoop greenhouses.

FARM TO TABLE

Shelburne Farms is perhaps Vermont's earliest example of the contemporary farm-to-table movement. It is a prime illustration of the growing trend to keep food—and the transportation of it—as local as possible. In the late 1980s, the early days of the restaurant at the Inn, few ingredients were available from nearby sources. Since then, there has been a significant increase in the use of ingredients harvested from the property. Shelburne Farms values its relationships with trusted, local food partners who supply such quality items as jams, honey, quail, turkey, and trout. Today, most of the restaurant's primary ingredients—vegetables, salad greens, fruits, eggs, herbs, meats, Cheddar cheese, and wild edibles—are grown, raised, or foraged on the property.

The restaurant and Vegetable Garden have a close and time-responsive relationship. What is harvested from the garden in the morning appears on the menu that night. From early July through September, nearly all of the vegetables and fruits the chefs need come directly from the garden. Beef and lamb also come from the farm. The restaurant purchases items such as baking staples and cooking oils from outside sources, but the executive chef makes it a priority to buy ingredients that are grown, raised, made, or processed in Vermont. This intimate food system is part of Shelburne Farms' mission and it provides diners with an expressive "taste of Vermont."

The restaurant is located at Shelburne House, which was restored as the Inn at Shelburne Farms in 1987. The dining room is the very room that Lila and Seward Webb dined in and graciously entertained family, friends, and guests over a century ago. One of the most beautiful dining rooms in

PAGE 226
On the first day of June, the restaurant chef prepared the Garden Greens Salad with the day's harvest from the Vegetable Garden: *hon tsai tai*, spinach, mesclun, and radish. He made a buttermilk ramp vinaigrette from wild leeks foraged on the property.

BELOW

The 1902 photograph of the dining room—the most formal room in Shelburne House—illustrates the furnishings and decor as it was designed for private use. The Webb family often entertained visiting guests and served several formal courses of French-style cuisine. The dining room opened up to a conservatory (far left), which was torn down in 1941 and its doorway covered over with bricks. Only two of the original Chippendale-style chairs remain in the collection today.

OPPOSITE

The restaurant staff sets the tables in the dining room for the arrival of guests. The neoclassical design of the dining room interior remains largely intact from Lila and Seward Webb's era, although their large dining table has been replaced with several smaller ones. The plasterwork ceiling, damask wall coverings, Vermont marble floors, floorboards, and mantel are all original. To the far left is an 1880 oil portrait of Lila Vanderbilt before she married Seward Webb, by Jules Joseph Lefebvre (1836–1911). The dining room is stately and elegant in appearance, but the restaurant encourages a less formal, come-as-you-are dress code.

the Northeast, it possesses some of the most dramatic and majestic views in Vermont. The dining room and its outdoor terrace face the southwest lawn of the Inn. The view is expansive and includes the Formal Gardens, the vast waters of Lake Champlain, and New York's Adirondack Mountains. As the evening sun sets behind the mountains, the sky overhead often fills with dazzling, colorful displays. When the night darkens, clear skies fill with bright stars. Inside, the grand room has changed very little, with the exception of the dispersal of some of the original furnishings. The wallcoverings, marble floor, fireplace, lighting, paintings, and several sculptures from Lila and Seward's era still remain. Despite its elegant ambiance, the restaurant evokes a relaxed atmosphere. Its welcoming, come-as-you-are, down-to-earth philosophy emanates through thoughtful, unfussy service and a menu of garden- and farm-fresh healthy dishes.

Like many rooms in Shelburne House, the dining room had gone through careful restoration to bring back the original turn-of-the-twentieth-century interior, but the chef's recipes from the Webbs' era were not revived. The Webbs enjoyed classic French cuisine and, being the style of the day, menus suggest they often served several courses over a long evening. That type of cuisine and dining does not fit with Shelburne Farms' character today. Instead, the menu is very direct and focuses on enhancing the taste and presentation of the ingredient, rather than manipulating or altering its taste. Unlike cooking styles that, for example, required peeling and shaping similar-sized carrots into multiple, identical disks and steeping them with a different flavor, the Inn's chefs serve fresh, baby carrots that might not be

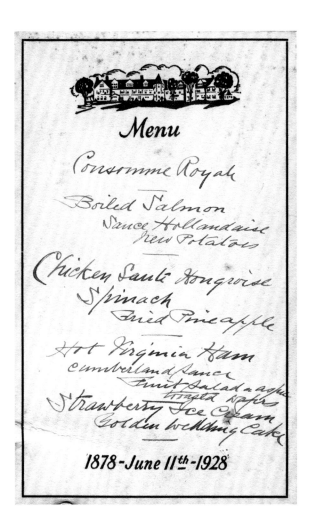

Menu

Consommé Royale

Boiled Salmon
Sauce Hollandaise
New Potatoes

Chicken Sauté Hongroise
Spinach
Fried Pineapple

Hot Virginia Ham
Cumberland Sauce
Fruit Salad a la [...]
[...] Wafers
Strawberry Ice Cream
Golden Wedding Cake

1878 - June 11th - 1928

LEFT

A June 11, 1928, dinner menu celebrates the fiftieth wedding anniversary of Lila and Seward's close friends, John "Jack" and Mary Purdy. On the reverse side is a poem written by Lila, which was possibly read on the occasion.

BELOW

Another photograph from 1902 shows a different angle of the dining room, with a more intimate arrangement of furniture, including upholstered straight-back chairs. The opening to the conservatory is seen to the far right. A large oriental carpet provided warmth to the room and helped to soften the sounds of merriment. The *torchères* remain in the room today.

OPPOSITE

A marble bust of Medusa by an unknown artist set against the vibrant red damask wall covering commands a presence on the Vermont marble mantel in the dining room. It has remained in the same location for over one hundred years. On cool days, a warm crackling fire in the fireplace greets diners.

BELOW

A group of family, friends, and longtime employees gather on the dining room terrace for a luncheon party to celebrate James Watson Webb's fiftieth birthday on July 1, 1934. Period photographs reveal that the awning over the terrace was always open during the warmer seasons, providing the family and their guests with shelter from the sun and a cool place to dine during the hot Vermont summers.

OPPOSITE

The dining room terrace provides guests with a cool, comfortable place to dine just as it did over a hundred years ago. Some of the iron tables and chairs are original (far right). The terrace was resurfaced with large pieces of bluestone during the comprehensive Shelburne House restoration, from 1985 to 1987. Today, the restaurant serves breakfast and dinner every day of the week, and a Sunday brunch.

perfectly formed. They will leave the skins on them because they are natural and tender; they'll serve them whole with a bit of the green stem remaining. There is integrity to the style that is wholesome and of the moment.

Having tremendous resources right on the property is certainly a great advantage. However, managing a well-run farm of this scale is a lot of responsibility and hard work. From the tending of seedlings in the greenhouses to the care of lambs born in the barn and calves raised in the pastures, the work requires the effort of several individuals as well as the cooperation of nature. These quality ingredients are slowly cultivated and managed in the sustainable, localized food system on Shelburne Farms' property.

One important part of cooking that goes unnoticed is what happens with the parts of ingredients that are not used for meals. In cooking, vegetable peels, leaves, stalks, and ends that are not destined for the plate are trimmed or cut off and placed in containers in the kitchen. At the end of each day, a large amount of vegetable matter accumulates. These "scraps" are used to make compost at one of the large composting areas. Combined with manure from the farm's animals and other organic matter, unused vegetable portions eventually turn into rich compost that each spring is spread on the fields, enriching the soil with new and essential ingredients. What started as a seed completes a circle of growth to ultimately enrich the land for another growing season.

With fresh ingredients straight from the farm, the cooks in the kitchen respond to the season. In early spring, before vegetables are mature, they will forage nettles, ramps, fiddleheads, and pheasant-back mushrooms

BELOW, LEFT

Each day, in the morning, several chefs meet to discuss what they will prepare for the evening meal.

BELOW, RIGHT

The executive chef composes Poached Pouch Egg and Mushrooms with Grits (see recipe on page 252).

OPPOSITE

Napa Cabbage Salad with radish, candied pecans, apple *gastrique*, herbed yogurt, scallion, and preserved vinaigrette is an example of the kind of salad served in June, depending on what is fresh from the Vegetable Garden. Over the course of the week, some of the ingredients might change, and with it the salad's flavors.

from the forest. Some foraged edibles make their way onto the dinner plate as a salad, with pasta, or alongside eggs for breakfast. When early spring greens and asparagus are harvested from the Vegetable Garden, they are prepared and served in a variety of ways for a week or two and remain on the menu until their growing time is over.

At Shelburne Farms' restaurant, the farm and garden ingredients are extremely tasty. And, the attractive presentation of food in a bowl, on a plate, in a glass, or on a serving board adds significantly to the overall dining experience. The subtle, final additions of fresh microgreens, finely chopped nuts, and sauces spark additional layers of unique flavor as well as visual interest.

The restaurant is open to Inn guests and the public from early May to mid-October—the most fertile growing season in Vermont. The executive chef's philosophy is to cook by intuition: he does not follow established, tried-and-true recipes. Creativity is an important part of his process. He and his team of chefs form menu ideas based on available farm and garden ingredients. Focusing on a certain item, such as lamb or broccoli, they pair tastes with accompaniments, such as hazelnuts with broccoli and basil with lamb. The chefs build out taste sensations from the ingredients and construct a menu for starters, salads, soups, vegetables, and main dishes. A menu comes together resourcefully and imaginatively as fresh ingredients come into season and make their way into the kitchen. The chefs might get enough of one ingredient that will last for as little as five days or as much as three weeks, and when they are gone, they will not be served again.

BELOW, LEFT
The restaurant's butcher prepares a section of lamb for the Trio of Shelburne Farms Lamb.

BELOW, RIGHT
The restaurant's Feast of the Field is an organic portrait of what grows in the Vegetable Garden and is foraged from the property. Each vegetable is individually prepared so that its unique character and taste are allowed to shine. The magnificent platter of vegetables is analogous to a charcuterie board of meats: The vegetables are prepared fresh, grilled, sautéed, roasted, or pickled. This dish can be shared among a few diners or served to a large party. The vegetables are arranged to resemble a farm landscape and placed on edible "dirt," made from dark brown bread that is seasoned, toasted, and then crumbled. As the growing season progresses and different vegetables become available, the Feast of the Field ingredients reflect the harvest of the day.

OPPOSITE
Trio of Shelburne Farms Lamb with golden raisin and apricot-hazelnut couscous, cucumber, kale, *tatsoi*, rhubarb puree, and port wine demi-glace.

The kitchen has moved away from serving a large piece of protein as the featured item in the middle of the plate. Instead, it breaks meats into smaller portions of different cuts and provides more vegetables from its Vegetable Garden around the smaller portions of meats. Rather than serve one big, eight-ounce portion of meat on a plate, the chefs will present a trio of beef, consisting of small portions of different cuts. Diners get a taste of filet, short rib, and a bit of roast, or—with lamb—braised lamb, sausage, and a chop. It is a great way to show the variety of a whole animal, and provides a broader taste experience.

A typical dinner menu offers a few choices each of appetizers, soups, salads, entrées, and desserts. An abundance of appealing items includes a bounty of food from the farm and Vegetable Garden. Buttermilk Cucumber Soup with ginger cream, cilantro, and charred scallion; Strawberry Salad with mesclun, spinach, Vermont chèvre, chive blossom, and lemon balm–ginger vinaigrette; Butcher Board with lamb summer sausage, chili beef sausage, chorizo, chicken sausage, and house pickles; Mint-Chèvre Gnocchi with scallion, snow peas, rhubarb, snap peas, and sesame seeds; Duo of Shelburne Farms Beef with charred scallion-potato salad, rainbow chard, radish puree, and charred spring onion are examples of the chefs' inventiveness, all of which are presented beautifully.

An inspiring example of a clear connection to place-based sustainability, dining at the Inn is the delicious endnote of a multifaceted story that blends together Shelburne Farms' mission.

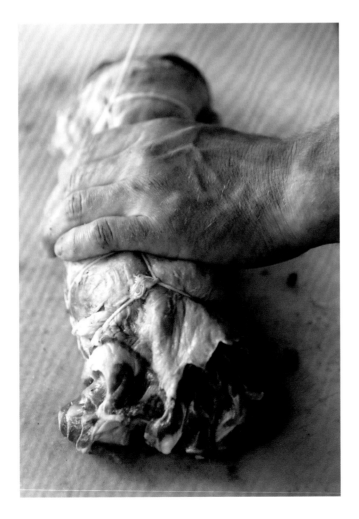

BELOW, LEFT
Early spring mint from the Vegetable Garden is the inspiration for the mint-infused cream and candied mint leaves for Spearmint Panna Cotta.

BELOW, RIGHT
Along one long, brick wall of the Formal Gardens outside the Inn is an herb garden planted for its variety of taste and color among the other, more dramatic flower borders in the garden "rooms." The chefs often pick fresh herbs from it to use as garnishes.

OPPOSITE
Spearmint Panna Cotta with strawberry gin granita, candied mint leaves, and juniper is a colorful dessert that combines the distinctive texture of the flaked, iced strawberry granita with the delicate and creamy panna cotta. It is an inviting early summer treat, tasting almost like a cocktail, and highlights two fresh and fragrant ingredients from the Vegetable Garden: spearmint and strawberries.

A Note About the Recipes

At the Inn's restaurant, because of the flexibility and spontaneity of cooking in response to the day, week, and month of harvesting in-season ingredients, the kitchen is not associated with "signature recipes." The dining experience is unique and exciting.

I asked the restaurant's executive chef to feature several dishes that exemplify Shelburne Farms' style of cooking and showcase homegrown ingredients. His procedures for the farm-to-table recipes that follow can be used as examples for the home cook. Note that these recipes do not necessarily rely on measurements for a specific outcome. However, in many instances measurements are given as a guide. All the preparation suggestions are based on general cooking techniques. Use the recipes as inspirational guides, follow your intuition, and be creative. The results will always be slightly different, and that is part of the recipes' appeal. Be sure to source the freshest and most trusted organic suppliers in your area to achieve the best flavor.

Farm-to-Table Recipes

Pantry Recipes

Pea Shoot Salad with Herb Vinaigrette and Radish Aioli

SERVES 4 AS A SIDE OR 2 AS A MAIN COURSE

Crisp, tender, and deliciously sweet, pea shoots are among the first greens to sprout in the Vegetable Garden's greenhouses in early spring. They are a staple ingredient on the Inn's menus throughout spring and well into summer, and are prepared in a variety of ways throughout the seasons. When they are fresh, the leaves, tendrils, and stems are delicate enough to eat raw. They can also be wilted or lightly stir-fried. The vegetable gardeners plant a few trays of pea seeds each week—when they sprout, the pea shoots are harvested for salads and other dishes. Some pea shoots are planted in the field gardens and grow to bear peas for consumption. Pea shoots—part of the legume family—are also sewn on the vegetable fields as a cover crop. Legumes take nitrogin naturally from the air and put it back in the soil, which improves soil fertility.

Prepare the Herb Vinaigrette and Radish Aioli ahead of making the salad so they are ready to toss on the fresh greens.

Make:
  Herb Vinaigrette (p. 276)
  Radish Aioli (p. 277)

In a salad bowl, combine:
  1 bunch pea shoots
  ¼ bunch chervil, chopped
  4 "Walking" onion tops, julienned
  ¼ pound Wrinkled Crinkle cress, chopped
  4 small radishes, thinly sliced with a microplane
Toss the salad with the Herb Vinaigrette.

TO SERVE

Brush a smear of Radish Aioli on a plate.
Arrange a portion of the dressed salad on top of the aioli.
Garnish with:
  Sunflower seeds, toasted
  Chive blossoms
  Freshly ground black pepper

Carrot-on-Carrot Salad with Black Walnuts and Black Walnut Vinaigrette

SERVES 2

This salad is a summer celebration of the color orange and the different tastes of carrots. The carrots are presented in three ways: raw, roasted, and emulsified. The Black Walnut Vinaigrette, combined with a garnish of fragrant, crushed, raw black walnuts, pairs well with the carrots. Shelburne Farms' black walnut trees produce a bounty of nuts, foraged in early autumn. A prolific, stately black walnut tree is located next to the new sugarhouse at the Vegetable Garden, where gathering basketfuls of nuts is easy.

CARROT EMULSION

Preheat the oven to 350°F.
Peel:
    1 pound baby orange carrots, well scrubbed and chopped
Place the carrots in a shallow baking dish and add:
    1 shallot, finely chopped
    1-inch piece fresh ginger, grated
    1 cup canola oil
    1 dried chipotle pepper, chopped
    ½ teaspoon salt
    2 tablespoons Shelburne Farms maple syrup
Cook covered in tinfoil and roast in the oven for 45 minutes, until the carrtos are tender.
Blend until smooth.
Transfer to a jar and refrigerate overnight.

ROASTED CARROTS

Preheat the oven to 350°F.
On a parchment-lined baking sheet, place:
    10 to 20 baby orange carrots with 1-inch stem remaining, well scrubbed
Drizzle with:
    Mild cooking oil
Using your hands, coat the carrots with the oil and sprinkle the carrots with salt.
Arrange them evenly spaced on the baking sheet and roast in the oven for 15 minutes, or until soft.
Cool before serving.

RAW CARROTS

Using a Japanese mandoline, slice:
    4 medium orange carrots, well scrubbed
Place the sliced carrots in a medium bowl and add:
    ¼ cup dried currants
    A handful of microgreens
Toss lightly with:
    Black Walnut Vinaigrette (p. 275)

TO SERVE

Make a pool of the carrot emulsion on a plate.
Arrange the whole roasted carrots on the carrot emulsion.
Top with a small handful of the dressed raw carrots.
Garnish with:
    Bits of fresh, raw black walnuts

Strawberry Gazpacho

SERVES 4 AS A SIDE OR 2 AS A MAIN COURSE

Shelburne Farms' strawberries are grown in the hoop greenhouses and produce fruit from early May through July. They are the predominate player in this orchestral gazpacho, giving it a complex, yet light, sweetness. The Moscato wine harmonizes with the flavors of the traditional ingredients, while enhancing the strawberries. For a more rustic gazpacho, puree the mixture for less time, leaving small chunks of strawberries and vegetables.

In a large bowl, combine:

    1¼ quarts strawberries, hulled and sliced into four to six pieces each

    1 jalapeño pepper (seeds removed if less heat is desired), roughly chopped into 1-inch pieces

    1 shallot, roughly chopped into ½-inch pieces

    1 large ripe red tomato, roughly cut into wedges

    1 red pepper, deveined, seeded, and roughly chopped into 1-inch pieces

    1 fennel bulb, trimmed and roughly chopped into ½-inch pieces

    1 spring onion, roughly chopped into ½-inch-long pieces

    ¼ cup sunflower seeds, toasted

    ¼ cup whole almonds, toasted

    1 garlic clove, finely chopped

    ¼ cup candied ginger

Stir in:

    2 tablespoons salt

Cover and let sit out for 1 hour (for the flavors to combine and to let the salt soften the vegetables).

Working in batches in a blender or food processor, combine the strawberry mixture with:

    ½ bottle (1½ cups) Moscato or other sweet sparkling wine

Blend until smooth.

Cool in the refrigerator.

TO SERVE

Place the cold gazpacho in individual bowls or stemmed glasses.

Garnish with:

    A drizzle of Green Herb Oil (p. 276)

    1 fennel frond or fresh mint leaves, coarsely chopped

    Crushed toasted almonds

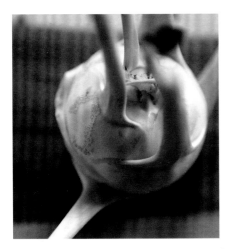

Smoked Cheddar and Maple Stout Soup

SERVES 4 AS A SIDE OR 2 AS A MAIN COURSE

Shelburne Farms' award-winning Cheddar cheese can be enjoyed sliced on its own or served on plain, crisp crackers, perhaps with a bit of honey and a fresh herb on top. During evening cocktails, the Inn offers sliced Cheddar cheese simply on its own. It is also a wonderful cooking ingredient. This picante soup calls for another Vermont-made product—Maple Breakfast Stout from the 14th Star Brewing Co. in St. Albans. The stout delectably balances the smoky flavor of the cheese and lightens the soup's creamy texture.

In a large saucepan, combine:
>   1 tablespoon vegetable oil
>   1 onion, chopped
>   1 shallot, chopped
>   5 garlic cloves, chopped
>   2 carrots, chopped
>   1 kohlrabi, peeled and chopped
>   3 potatoes, peeled and chopped
>   5 sprigs thyme, stemmed
>   ½ teaspoon salt

Place over medium heat to sweat the vegetables for a few minutes.
Add:
>   1 pint Maple Breakfast Stout
>   3 cups water

Bring to a simmer and cook for about 20 minutes, until the vegetables are soft.
Remove from the heat and transfer to a blender.
Add:
>   1 pound Shelburne Farms smoked Cheddar cheese or other good-quality smoked Cheddar, grated
>   1 tablespoon sherry vinegar
>   2 tablespoons honey
>   1 teaspoon ground Aleppo pepper

Puree until smooth.

TO SERVE

Place the soup in individual bowls.
Garnish with:
>   Mustard greens, wilted
>   Pepitas, toasted
>   Cumin seeds, toasted

Poached Pouch Eggs with Mushrooms and Grits

SERVES 4

When poaching eggs, the fresher the egg, the better the taste. The farms' flock of russet red hens provides the Inn's kitchen with several dozen eggs daily. The eggs can be poached ahead of time and refrigerated for up to 48 hours if desired. (Reheat in warm water before serving.) To make grits, the Inn's chef uses water instead of the more traditional milk to allow the flavor of the rich heirloom painted corn grown at the Vegetable Garden shine through. He recommends grinding the corn right before cooking the grits.

EGG POUCHES

Line a small bowl with plastic wrap and brush with oil.
Into the plastic-lined bowl, break:
    1 large egg
Add:
    A pinch of salt and pepper
Carefully bring the sides of the plastic wrap up around the
    egg to form a small pouch.
Tie the pouch with kitchen twine to seal it.
Repeat with 3 more eggs.
Set the egg pouches aside.

GRITS

Combine in a saucepan:
    1 cup freshly ground cornmeal
    1 shallot, minced
    4½ cups water
Bring to a boil.
Stir with a wooden spoon over medium heat for 10 to 12
    minutes, until thick and creamy.
Add:
    ¼ cup grated Shelburne Farms Cheddar cheese or other
        good-quality Cheddar
    Salt to taste

POACHED EGGS

Cook the eggs in their pouches in boiling water for 5 minutes.
Remove the egg pouches from the boiling water and set aside
    and let cool to room temperature.

TO SERVE

Place the grits in individual bowls.
Over the grits, place a few marinated mushrooms from:
    Mushroom Conserva (p. 276)
Remove the plastic wrap from the eggs and place 1 egg on
    each serving.
Garnish with:
    Microgreens, lightly tossed with a flavorful oil

Beet Soufflés with Goat Cheese

SERVES 6

The farms' eggs, beets, and maple syrup are the primary ingredients in this vibrant twist on a French soufflé that can be served hot or cold. The earthy, dark-red beets are combined with fresh eggs and made into mini soufflés that are placed on a creamy white goat cheese spread. It is a flavorful and visual delight.

SOUFFLÉS

Preheat the oven to 350°F.
Butter six small soufflé dishes and set aside.
In a large pot, place:
>   2 pounds beets, peeled and cubed

Cover the beets with water and bring to a boil over high heat.
Cook until tender, about 15 minutes.
Drain well.
Transfer to a bowl and mash (or puree in a food processor).
Set aside.
In a medium bowl, combine:
>   3 large eggs
>   ½ cup maple syrup
>   2 ounces (4 tablespoons) unsalted butter, melted
>   3 tablespoons all-purpose flour
>   ¼ teaspoon baking powder
>   ½ teaspoon grated orange zest

Whisk the ingredients together.
Add the mashed beets and mix well.
Fill the prepared soufflé dishes with the batter.
Bake until the tops are set, about 30 minutes.
Let cool to room temperature and carefully unmold.

GOAT CHEESE SPREAD

Combine in a medium bowl:
>   ½ cup chèvre (goat cheese)
>   3 tablespoons whole milk
>   A pinch of salt

Mix together with a fork to make a creamy spread.

TO SERVE

Smear a generous amount of the goat cheese spread on
    individual plates.
Place an unmolded beet soufflé on the goat cheese in the
    center.
Garnish with:
>   Microgreens or thinly sliced arugula, lightly dressed
>   Pepitas, toasted

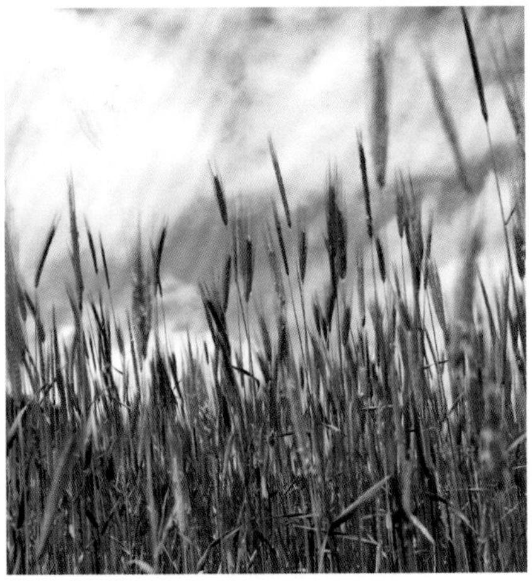
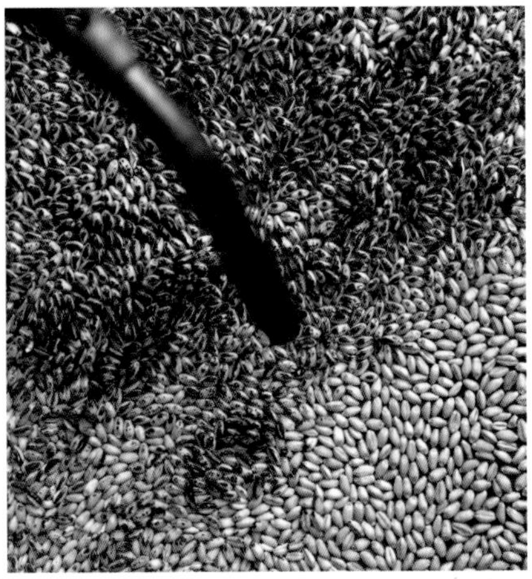
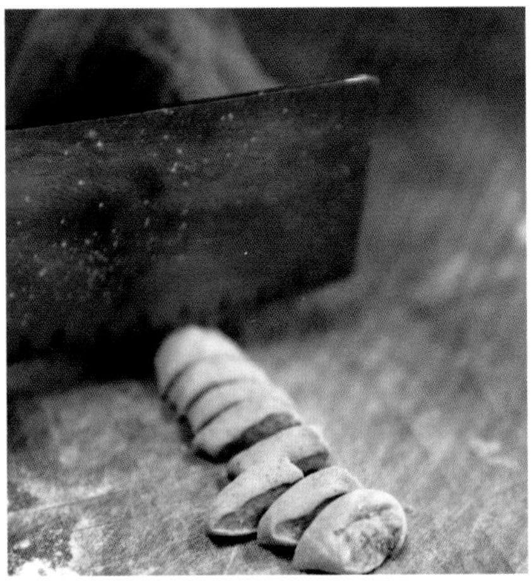
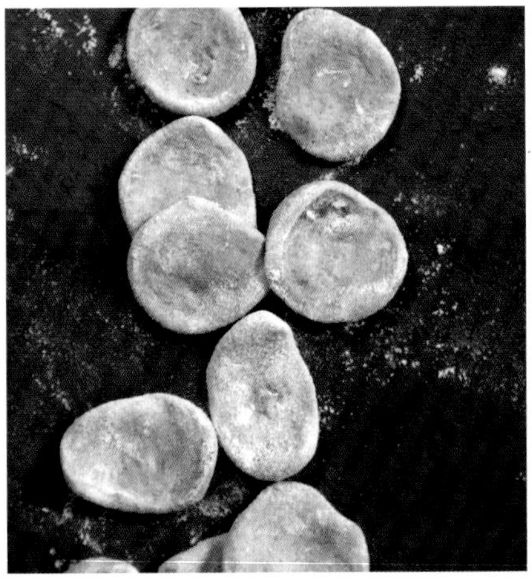

Homemade Orecchiette with Grano Arso

SERVES 4

Grano arso *means "burnt wheat." This traditional Italian recipe is inspired from the period when gleaners were allowed to forage grain from burnt fields after a harvest. The pasta that results from burnt wheat is delicious, with a nutty, smoky, earthy flavor. Making orecchiette does not require a pasta machine, so it is very easy for the home cook. The fresh orecchiette is dressed with pan-charred onions that accentuate the toasted wheat flavor; a few garden fresh vegetables and a simple cheese sauce complete the dish.*

HOMEMADE ORECCHIETTE

On a metal baking sheet, place:
- ½ cup unground whole wheat berries

With a culinary torch (or under the broiler), gently toast the wheat berries until most are slightly blackened.
Shake the pan to turn the wheat berries, and torch again gently.
Transfer the burnt wheat berries to a flour mill or blender and grind into flour.
Place the grano arso flour in a large bowl and add:
- 1½ cups semolina flour

Combine the flours together, adding:
- ¾ cup water

Using your hands, mix to form a dough.
On a clean wooden board, knead the dough for about 5 minutes, until it is soft and smooth.
Cover the dough with a bowl and let rest for 30 minutes. (At this stage, the dough can be frozen and used at a later time.)
Divide the dough into about four egg-size portions.
On a lightly floured board, roll each portion into a snake of dough about 1 inch in diameter.
Slice the snakes into ½-inch-thick disks.
Place each disk cut side up and make a thumbprint in the disk, gently rolling your thumb on the pasta to create a little ridge on the outer rim.
(continued)

CHEESE SAUCE

Combine in a Vitamix or other high speed blender:
> 1 pound two- or three-year-old Shelburne Farms
>   Cheddar cheese, or other good-quality Cheddar,
>   grated
> 1 pound cherry tomatoes
> A pinch of salt

Puree for about 2 minutes, until the first waft of steam rises out of the Vitamix (when it is warm enough to create the desired consistency).

CHARRED ONIONS

In a sauté pan, combine:
> 2 tablespoons canola oil
> 1 cup cipollini onions, halved

Place the onions cut side down and sear over high heat for a few minutes, until browned, almost charred.

While the onions are searing, bring a pot of heavily salted water to a boil (¾ cup salt per gallon of water).

When the onions are cooked, splash a little of the boiling salty water over them.

TO COOK THE PASTA

Add the orecchiette to the boiling water and cook for about 1 minute.

Add:
> 1 cup green beans, sliced into 1-inch-long pieces

Cook the pasta and beans for about 30 seconds more.

Drain and transfer to the pan with the onions.

Briefly stir and then add ½ cup of the cheese sauce (or more to taste).

Stir in:
> 1 cup cherry tomatoes, sliced in half

TO SERVE

Smear individual plates or pasta bowls with:
> Green Herb Couli (p. 276)

Place the cooked orecchiette mixture on top.

Garnish with:
> Fresh edible flowers, such as nasturtiums or day lillies
> Fresh soft herbs, such as basil, oregano, or parsley

Lamb and Cheddar Meatballs
with Pickled Wild Leeks

SERVES 4 AS A SIDE OR 2 AS A MAIN COURSE

Each year, one-hundred-plus grass-fed lambs raised on Shelburne Farms' property are processed for their meat. The Inn's kitchen uses approximately ninety of these lambs as a featured ingredient in its dishes. The remainder is sold at the Shelburne Farms' store. This easy-to-prepare country-style meatball recipe combines ground lamb with another one of the farm's notable food products: Cheddar cheese. The chef uses quinoa flour as a binder to hold the meatballs firmly together (and keep them gluten free). Pickled wild leeks are a tasty and colorful way to elevate the meatball to another level.

MEATBALLS

Preheat the oven to 350°F.
Place in a mixing bowl or food processor:
    ¼ cup quinoa flour
    1 pound lamb, ground
    2 teaspoons oregano
    1 teaspoon rosemary
    1 teaspoon savory
    ¼ pound two-year Shelburne Farms Cheddar cheese, or
        other good-quality Cheddar, grated
    1 spring onion, minced
    2 tablespoons salt
    1 teaspoon freshly ground pepper
Blend together all the ingredients, using your hands or a food processor with the paddle attachment.
Use an ice cream scoop to create about 20 uniform (1-ounce) meatballs, and then with your hands tightly roll into round balls.
Place the meatballs on a parchment-lined baking sheet and bake for 12 minutes.

TO SERVE

With a rustic stick or toothpick, skewer each meatball with a:
    Pickled Wild Leek (p. 277)
Arrange the meatballs on a wooden board or plate and sprinkle lightly with:
    Microgreens

Pheasant-Back-Mushroom Carpaccio with Nettle Pesto

SERVES 2

Shelburne Farms' woodlands are full of wild edibles. After a cold rain and a few warm days in the spring, morels—prized for their delicious taste—bloom and are plentiful, but hard to find. Mushroom hunters look for the distinctive honeycomb-like capped fungi on the forest floor. Pheasant-back mushrooms, which fruit at the same time, are a little easier to locate; they often grow out of dead elm tree logs and also thrive on living maple trees. The mushroom is commonly called pheasant-back because of the pattern of colors that is similar to that of the stately bird's back.

Marinate the mushrooms a day ahead of serving, using a mild olive oil—not extra virgin, which would overpower the delicate flavor and watermelon-like aroma.

Clean and set aside:
   2 medium-size, freshly foraged pheasant-back
      mushrooms
On a small piece of cheesecloth, combine:
   3 bay leaves
   3 dried chilies, chopped
   1 tablespoon mustard seeds
   1 tablespoon black peppercorns
   1 tablespoon Aleppo red pepper
Roll the cheesecloth around the spices and tie the ends
   together with kitchen twine to create a small satchel
   (bouquet garni).
In a medium saucepan, combine:
   1½ cups mild olive oil
   2 sprigs fresh thyme
   2 whole garlic cloves
Heat the oil mixture over medium heat until the garlic starts
   to sizzle.
Add the cleaned mushrooms and bouquet garni, along with:
   1 teaspoon sherry vinegar
   1 shallot, finely chopped
   ¼ teaspoon salt
Gently stir the mushrooms in the sizzling oil for a few
   minutes, until tender.
Let cool.
Transfer the mushrooms and oil to a glass or ceramic bowl
   and cover with plastic wrap, or into a Mason jar, and
   marinate overnight in the refrigerator.

TO SERVE

On individual plates, smear across the surface:
   A few spoonfuls of Nettle Pesto (p. 277)
Remove the marinated mushrooms from the oil. Thinly slice
   the mushrooms and blot dry with paper towels.
Place the sliced mushrooms on the pesto and garnish with:
   Shelburne Farms Clothbound Cheddar cheese, or other
      good quality Cheddar, grated
   Crispy shallots
   Pickled Mustard Seeds (p. 277)
   Chili Oil (p. 276)
   Microgreens

Duo of Shelburne Farms Beef

Each year, more than a dozen of the Dairy Farm's calves are raised for beef. (All the pasture-raised beef served at the Inn is raised on the farm.) When they reach maturity, they roam as a herd on the property's pastures, feeding on green grass and meadow plants. The chef strives to use parts from the whole animal—not just the special cuts—to create interesting flavors, combinations, and textures when cooking them.

This main dish, providing a presentation idea and giving suggested accompaniments, calls for two cuts of beef and two cooking methods. The top portion is a steak, grilled simply with salt and pepper. The bottom portion is a roast, baked with a garlic herb rub in a 200°F oven—not hot enough to sear the meat, but warm enough to cook it slowly to achieve the tender, pink consistency (the cooking time depends on the weight and size of the cut).

The chef creates a meal by integrating other fresh ingredients into the dish, which vary throughout the season depending on their freshness. The simple preparation of the beef combined with a classic bárnaise sauce, garden vegetables, such as sautéed rainbow chard stems, crispy potato salad, radish puree, and braised greens, is rustic country fare made sublime.

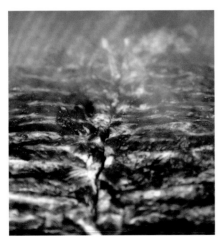

Slow-Roasted Pork Ribs with Barbeque Spice Rub and Blueberry Barbeque Sauce

SERVING DEPENDS ON THE AMOUNT OF PORK RIBS

The pork ribs used for this recipe were from a large three-year-old sow that weighed between 800 and 900 pounds. The sow's meat had a deep porky flavor and a color almost as dark as beef. The chef wanted to do something special with the ribs. He created a smoked- and slow-roasted method to further accentuate the richness of the pork's flavor. He made several dozen pork ribs from the meat butchered from the sow. At home, turn to this recipe for the chef's cooking process by using store-bought pork ribs with the Inn's recipes for a spice rub and barbeque sauce (p. 275). Adjust the quantity of ribs to the amount you wish to serve as either an appetizer or main course.

For the barbeque sauce, if blueberries are not in season the chef recommends using strawberries, raspberries, currants, or seaberries instead. Adjust the amount (and type) of sugar when making the sauce, depending on the sweetness of the fruit. He encourages experimenting with different vinegars—balsamic, white balsamic, white wine vinegar—to create your own sauce.

If you have a smoker, cold smoke the ribs for 45 minutes before roasting the pork ribs in the oven.

Preheat the oven to 200°F.

On a rack in a deep roasting pan, place:
　Pork ribs

In a mixing bowl, combine ¼ cup of the ground chilies with:
　1 pound maple granules (or brown sugar)
　½ pound salt
　¼ cup barbeque spice rub

Using a large whisk, mix the ingredients together.

Store the rub in a tightly sealed jar in the refrigerator for 2 to 3 months.

Coat all sides of the ribs with:
　Barbeque Spice Rub (p. 275)

Fill the roasting pan with about 1 inch of water.

Cover the pan with tinfoil and poke several dime-size holes (so the ribs will not steam when they are roasting, but will not dry out too much).

Roast for about 12 hours.

Brush with:
　Blueberry Barbeque Sauce (p. 275)

TO SERVE

Onto a large serving platter, smear a generous amount of the barbeque sauce.

Cut the ribs apart and place on the serving platter.

Sprinkle lightly with:
　Microgreens

Maple Tarts with Candied Spruce Tips

SERVES 8

These mini dessert tarts are made with Shelburne Farms' maple syrup and served with a tahini ganache, toasted black sesame seeds, and maple candy. Tender spruce tips are fresh for only about a week and a half in the spring. In Vermont, they are usually ready to pick some time during the last two weeks of May through the first week of June. Freshness will vary depending on location and climate zone. Readiness is easily identified as follows: Last year's growth is dark green, and the new growth is unmistakably bright green. For this recipe, the spruce tips are candied and presented whole, adding a delicate visual pleasure with their exciting flavor.

MAPLE FILLING

In a bowl, combine:
    1 cup packed brown sugar
    ½ cup maple syrup
    ½ cup buttermilk
    ½ cup unsalted butter, melted
    4 large eggs
    1 tablespoon cornmeal
    1 teaspoon vanilla
    A pinch of salt
Whisk together until smooth.
Strain the filling through a sieve into a pitcher, pressing the last thick bits through with a spoon.

TART CRUST

In a food processor, combine:
    Slightly less than 1 cup (204 grams) all-purpose flour
    ¼ cup (60 grams) powdered sugar
    ¼ teaspoon salt
    8½ tablespoons (128 grams) unsalted butter, cold
Process until the ingredients have a sandy texture.
Add:
    1 large egg yolk
Process until the dough begins to come together.
Portion the dough into 8 individual 3½-inch tart tins and press onto the bottoms and up the sides to create tart shells.
Freeze the shells for 30 minutes.
Preheat the oven to 350°F.
Blind-bake the tart shells until lightly brown, 10 to 12 minutes.
Let cool.
Fill the shells with the maple filling and bake until the filling is set, about 15 minutes.
Let cool.

TO SERVE

Using a pastry palate knife or spatula, make a smear on each individual plate with:
    Tahini Ganache (p. 227)
Garnish the ganache with:
    Maple candy, crushed
    Black sesame seeds, toasted
Place a cooled maple tart on the ganache and carefully top with a few:
    Candied Spruce Tips (p. 275)
Serve immediately.

Rhubarb Sage Crostatas

Rhubarb is traditionally a harbinger of spring—its vibrant sour flavor and bright pink color give it a distinctive personality. Long rows of rhubarb grow at the Vegetable Garden. A crostata is an open tartlet with a buttery crust and fruit or other filling. A jam made from tart rhubarb and savory sage combines with diced raw rhubarb to make a delicious filling for these crostatas. Buttermilk ice cream is a nice counterpoint to the sharpness of the rhubarb and pepper-infused honey adds a delightful sweet drizzle.

CROSTATA DOUGH

In a food processor, combine:
> 1¼ cups (315 grams) all-purpose flour
> ½ teaspoon salt
> 15 tablespoons (225 grams) unsalted butter

Briefly pulse to achieve a sandy texture.

In a bowl, whisk together:
> ½ cup (120 grams) crème fraîche
> 1 tablespoon white vinegar
> ⅓ cup ice water

Add to the flour mixture in the food processor and process until the dough begins to come together, adding more ice water as needed.

Place the dough on a lightly floured board. Form into a ball, cover with plastic wrap, and chill for at least 2 hours.

RAW RHUBRARB

In a bowl, combine:
> 1 cup diced rhubarb
> 2 teaspoons grated lemon zest
> 1 teaspoon slivered fresh sage

CROSTATAS

Preheat the oven to 350°F.

On a floured board, roll out the dough to ⅜ inch thick.

Cut out circles of dough, approximately 4 inches in diameter.

Form dough cups by raising and pinching the edges together in four places, making pleats.

Fill the cups with:
> Rhubarb Sage Jam (p. 277)

Dust with:
> Cornstarch

Top each crostata with raw diced rhubarb.

In a small bowl, combine:
> 1 egg yolk
> 2 tablespoons heavy cream

Brush the edges of the crostata with the yolk wash.

Bake the crostatas for 20 to 30 minutes.

Let cool.

TO SERVE

Drizzle on individual plates:
> Pepper Honey (p. 277)

Place the crostatas on the honey.

Beside each crostata, place a scoop of:
> Buttermilk ice cream

Garnish with:
> Toasted pecans

Serve immediately.

Seaberry Sorbet

SERVES 8 (MAKES 1 QUART)

Seaberry, also called sea buckthorn, produces clusters of small brilliant orange berries on tall shrubs. Seaberry bushes are grown at the Vegetable Garden in the orchard, along with elderberry, black currants, raspberries, and several more delectable soft fruits. Eaten alone, the seaberry is quite astringent and sour, but with the addition of sugar the berry's flavor is transformed into a refreshing tropical-tasting citrusy treat. Sorbet is always refreshing after a meal. Adding flowers and candied fruits or vegetables makes this dessert a small and colorful work of art.

Combine in a bowl:
> 2 pounds seaberry pulp/juice
> 1 cup sugar

Stir to dissolve the sugar.
Freeze in an ice-cream maker.

TO SERVE

Place two scoops of the sorbet in an individual serving bowl
> or stemmed glass.

Garnish with:
> Candied black radish (optional)
> Pansy blossoms (or other edible flowers)

The Inn's Pantry recipes are micro recipes, used in some of the preceding Farm-to-Table recipes. They can be made ahead of time, stored, and used for other dishes you create.

Barbeque Spice Rub

MAKES 2 CUPS

Preheat the oven to 300°F.
On a medium baking sheet, spread out:
    2 ancho peppers
    3 casabel peppers
    3 chipotle peppers
    2 pasilla peppers
    ½ cup whole cumin seeds
    3 star anise
    ¼ teaspoon fennel seeds
Bake the dried chili mixture in the oven for about 5 minutes to dry further and begin to release the chilies' fragrance.
Transfer the mixture to a spice grinder and add:
    2 teaspoons mace
    2 tablespoons ground Aleppo pepper
Grind to a fine powder.
Transfer the ground chilies to a container.

Black Walnut Vinaigrette

MAKES 2 CUPS

Place in a blender:
    ½ cup black walnuts
Blend until finely chopped.
Add:
    ½ cup sherry vinegar
    ½ cup water
    ¼ cup honey
    ¼ teaspoon salt
Blend to combine.
Add:
    ½ cup mild olive oil
Blend to combine and thicken.
Store in a tightly sealed jar in the refrigerator for up to 1 week.

Blueberry Barbeque Sauce

MAKES 2 CUPS

Combine in a medium saucepan:
    1 pint blueberries
    2 shallots, chopped
    2 inch-piece fresh ginger, peeled and chopped
    ¾ cup red wine
    ¼ cup red wine vinegar
    ½ cup brown sugar
    1½ tablespoons salt
Bring to a boil over medium heat.
Simmer gently for 5 to 6 minutes, until slightly reduced and thickened.
Remove from the heat and add:
    2 tablespoons ground chilies from Barbeque Spice Rub (left)
Stir to combine.
Puree the sauce in a blender.
Store in a tightly sealed jar in the refrigerator for up to 1 week.

Candied Spruce Tips

MAKES 24 TO 30 TIPS

Line a baking sheet with a Silpat mat.
Pick and set aside:
    24 to 30 spruce tips, fresh, clean, and perfectly formed
In a medium bowl, add:
    1½ cup sugar
In another bowl, combine:
    1 large egg white
    ½ teaspoon cold water
Using your fingers instead of a whisk (so you don't create bubbles), break up the egg white globs.
Take a spruce tip and gently coat it with the egg white wash (the goal is to coat, not drench, the tip).
Place the tip in the bowl of sugar and gently toss to coat. Place on the lined baking sheet.
Repeat with the remaining tips.
Place the sugar-coated spruce tips in a dehydrator for 2 hours, until dry. (If you don't have a dehydrator, dry in a barely warm oven for several hours, checking often.)
Store in an airtight container for up to 2 days.

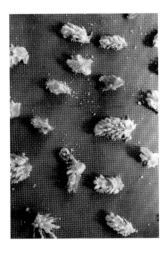

Chili Oil

MAKES 2 CUPS

In a medium saucepan, combine:
    2 cups mild olive oil
    2 tablespoons smoked paprika
    2 chili peppers, chopped with seeds
    2 cloves garlic, finely chopped
    4 sprigs thyme
    1 bay leaf
Simmer over medium low heat for 2 to 3
    minutes.
Strain through a sieve lined with a coffee
    filter into a medium bowl or container.
Store in a tightly sealed jar in the refrigerator
    for up to 4 weeks.

Green Herb Couli

MAKES ½ CUP

In a pot of boiling water, briefly blanch:
    ½ bunch parsley
    ¼ bunch chives
    ¼ bunch basil
Drain.
Transfer the herbs to a blender and add:
    ½ cup water
Blend until very smooth.
Strain off the solids using a fine mesh
    strainer.
Return the liquid to the blender and add:
    ¼ teaspoon xanthan gum
Blend until smooth.
Store in a tightly sealed jar in the refrigerator.
    For the freshest flavor, use within 2 or 3
    days.

Green Herb Oil

MAKES 2 CUPS

In a blender, place:
    1 bunch chives
    ½ bunch flat-leaf parsley
    ½ bunch basil
Place a small saucepan over medium-high
    heat and add:
    2 cups olive oil
Heat the oil to 350°F. (If you do not have a
    thermometer, toss a small piece of bread
    in the hot oil. If it browns in 10 seconds,
    the temperature is correct.)
Remove the oil from the heat and carefully
    pour over the herbs in the blender.
Puree until smooth.
Strain the herb oil through a sieve lined with
    a coffee filter.
Store in a tightly sealed jar in the refrigerator
    for up to 4 weeks.

Herb Vinaigrette

MAKES 2½ CUPS

In a medium bowl, combine:
    6 chives, finely chopped
    ½ bunch mint, finely chopped
    ½ bunch chervil, finely chopped
    ¼ bunch oregano, finely chopped
    2 tablespoons Dijon mustard
    2 tablespoons sugar
    1 cup white balsamic vinegar
    Salt to taste
Whisk together to thoroughly combine and
    dissolve the sugar and salt.
Continue to whisk while drizzling in:
    1 cup mild olive oil
Store in a tightly sealed jar in the refrigerator
    for up to 2 weeks.

Mushroom Conserva

MAKES 2 CUPS

Clean:
    ¼ pound freshly foraged or small
        cultivated mushrooms
Set aside.
On a small piece of cheesecloth, combine:
    3 bay leaves
    1 tablespoon mustard seeds
    3 dried chilies
    1 tablespoon black peppercorns
    1 tablespoon ground Aleppo pepper
Wrap the cheesecloth around the spices and
    tie the ends together with kitchen twine
    to create a small satchel (bouquet garni).
Place the bouquet garni in a medium
    saucepan and add:
    1½ cups mild olive oil
    2 sprigs thyme
    2 peeled garlic cloves
    ¼ teaspoon salt
Heat the oil over medium heat until the garlic
    starts to sizzle.
Lower the heat and gently simmer for about 7
    to 8 minutes, until tender.
Add:
    1 teaspoon sherry vinegar
    1 shallot, finely chopped
Stir the mushrooms into the oil and simmer
    for a few minutes to cook and shrink
    them.
Remove the bouquet garni and discard.
Transfer the cooked mushroom-oil mixture
    to a jar and seal. Invert and let cool to
    room temperature.
Let the mushrooms marinate overnight at
    room temperature.
Store in a tightly sealed jar in the refrigerator
    for up to 1 month.

Nettle Pesto

MAKES 2 CUPS

In a blender or food processor, combine:
    ½ pound nettles
    1 cup vegetable oil
    ¼ cup sunflower oil
    2 ounces Shelburne Farms Cheddar
        cheese, chopped
    1 teaspoon coriander
    1 garlic clove, peeled
    ½ teaspoon salt
Process until desired consistency, either
    slightly coarse for a rustic pesto or totally
    smooth for a more refined pesto.
Store in a tightly sealed jar in the refrigerator
    for up to 1 week.

Pepper Honey

MAKES ½ CUP

Using a mortar and pestle, grind very finely:
    ½ teaspoon black peppercorns
    ½ teaspoon white peppercorns
    ½ teaspoon pink peppercorns
Sieve the ground peppercorns to remove any
    large bits.
Transfer to a medium saucepan and add:
    ½ cup honey
Heat gently over medium-low heat for about
    5 minutes to allow the pepper to perfume
    the honey.
Let cool.
Store in a tightly sealed jar and keep at room
    temperature for up to four weeks.

Pickled Mustard Seeds

MAKES 1 CUP

In a saucepan, combine:
    1 cup brown or yellow mustard seeds
    1 cup sherry vinegar
    1 cup sugar
    1 teaspoon salt
Gently reduce over medium-low heat until
    the liquid is mostly gone and the mustard
    seeds are surrounded by a sweet and sour
    syrup, about 20 minutes.
Store in a tightly sealed jar in the refrigerator
    for up to 6 months.

Pickled Wild Leeks

MAKES 2 CUPS

Fill a Mason jar with:
    About 2 pounds wild leeks, cleaned and
        trimmed
In a small saucepan, combine:
    1 cup apple cider vinegar
    1 cup water
    ½ cup sugar
    3 tablespoons salt
    1 bay leaf
    1 teaspoon coriander seeds
    1 teaspoon black peppercorns
    1 teaspoon ground turmeric
Bring to a boil and simmer for several
    minutes to make a brine.
Pour the hot brine over the wild leeks. Seal
    the jar and invert.
Let cool to room temperature.
Store in the tightly sealed Mason jar in the
    refrigerator for up to 1 month.

Radish Aioli

MAKES 2½ CUPS

In the bowl of a food processor, combine:
    2 radishes, grated
    3 large egg whites
    2 tablespoons white balsamic vinegar
    1 tablespoon Dijon mustard
    1 tablespoon honey
    A pinch of salt
Process until smooth.
Continue to process while drizzling in:
    2 cups mild olive oil
Process until the oil is fully incorporated.
Store in a tightly sealed jar in the refrigerator
    for up to 1 week.

Rhubarb Sage Jam

MAKES 1 QUART

In a saucepan, combine:
    4 cups diced rhubarb
    ½ cup packed brown sugar
    1 tablespoon grated lemon zest
    2 tablespoons fresh sage leaves, slivered
Heat to a simmer over medium heat and cook
    for 10 to 15 minutes, until the rhubarb is
    soft and the mixture has thickened.
Let cool.
Store in a tightly sealed jar in the refrigerator
    for up to 2 weeks.

Tahini Ganache

MAKES 3 CUPS

In a saucepan, combine:
    ⅔ pound white chocolate, chopped
    3¼ tablespoons unsalted butter
Melt together over low heat.
Transfer to a blender and add:
    ¼ cup maple syrup
Blend briefly, then drizzle in:
    ½ cup heavy cream
Blend briefly, then add:
    ½ cup + 2 tablespoons tahini
    2 teaspoons salt
Blend until smooth.
Set aside in an airtight container until ready
    to use. It is best if used fresh.

AFTERWORD

Megan Camp

Shelburne Farms has touched the lives of many people, including me. When I was first introduced to Shelburne Farms in 1982, it was still a young nonprofit organization with lots of hope and vision for the future. I was in my twenties and an idealistic educator, passionate about making a difference in the world. I had grown up during the Civil Rights Movement of the 1960s in Washington, D.C., experienced the power of the first Earth Day, and felt a deep civic responsibility to help "save the planet." My professional aspirations were deeply rooted in my parents' lifelong commitment to education and social justice. I grew up believing—and remain convinced—that education plays an essential role in transforming society. The desire I felt for making change and the ethos of Shelburne Farms were a perfect match for my work to come.

In the early 1980s, I was studying at the University of Vermont in Burlington with a self-designed major in environmental studies and was writing my thesis on a "new paradigm for education" when my advisor recommended that I include an internship at Shelburne Farms as part of my research. In those days, you could not hop onto the Internet to learn about an organization, so I called Shelburne Farms to set up an appointment and rode my bike through the growing development along Route 7, six miles south, to Shelburne. As I pedaled onto the property, I thought I had been transported to another world and time. It was early spring, the pastures were just turning green, and the trees were budding. A school bus passed me, full of students arriving for a field trip to explore spring by searching for ephemeral wildflowers in the woods, helping to plant seeds in

The natural and agricultural landscape at Shelburne Farms is maintained through a strong commitment to land stewardship.

OPPOSITE

The natural world is a significant part of Shelburne Farms' living classroom, where students and visitors are inspired to create a cleaner and healthier world.

Years ago, American bald eagles were a rare sight; today, the magnificent birds are seen frequently (top right) soaring above the property and Lake Champlain.

the greenhouses, and marveling at newborn calves in the barn. Shelburne Farms was not the typical Vermont farm I had imagined, and nothing had prepared me for what I experienced during that first encounter. To this day, every time I pass through the gates, I feel the same awe, but now it is coupled with gratitude and love. My internship led to a position on Shelburne Farms' education staff, and I am blessed to still be part of a team that is nurturing the growth of this unique organization and helping to cultivate its work of educating for a sustainable future.

Shelburne Farms is a place with purpose. It is part of an international groundswell of people and organizations dedicated to shaping a better world. Education—rooted in a deep love of place—is our means to this end. As we prepare young people to be global citizens, we envision a healthy and just world rooted in diverse, caring, and resilient communities. Shelburne Farms is a place and an institution that is inspiring. It challenges and supports students, educators, families, and leaders to grapple with the big question of how to live responsibly in the twenty-first century.

Our home campus—a 1,400-acre working farm and forest—creates a real-world classroom where the big ideas of sustainability come alive every day. Stories that take place on the farm, such as "forest to furniture," "farm to plate," and "sun to cheese," give new and relevant meaning to the big ideas of "sustainability." For us, sustainability means practicing a shared responsibility for improving the quality of life for all—economically, socially, and environmentally—now, and for future generations. This is what guides the stewardship of our working landscape and historic property and knits together all the experiences we offer.

Sustainability is integrated into our education programs for all audiences, from four-year-old preschoolers discovering where their food comes from to ninety-year-old adults deepening their understanding of human impact on climate change. We link inquiry, knowledge, and action, and encourage learners to understand concepts, not just memorize them. Shelburne Farms is committed to the long haul. Every aspect of life is an opportunity to learn about and inspire sustainability: how food is grown, how energy and water are used, how we shape our living environment, and how we govern ourselves.

Shelburne Farms has become a vibrant center for learning and an incubator for new teaching strategies. Throughout the four seasons, joyful voices of school-age children echo from the farmyards, shores, fields, and forests. For our early learners, simple experiences like collecting eggs and sampling sweet maple sap directly from the tree cultivate joy and wonder. As children grow older, experiences such as taste testing and learning to cook local foods or studying how to conduct a renewable energy audit empower students to make a difference. Each year, 145,000 people visit Shelburne Farms to explore the land; make connections between nature, food, and community; and experience the beauty and spirit of the farm.

A growing audience for our programs is educators. By working with teachers we can extend our impact. Educators from all over the country and the world come to Shelburne Farms to participate in daylong workshops, residential weeklong institutes, and yearlong graduate-level programs. Our programs energize and support educators in weaving the concept of

OPPOSITE

Education starts at the Farm Barn, children's farm-yard, and at other locations on the property such as at the Vegetable Garden. Through education programs and hands-on work and activities, students and visitors of all ages take lessons home and put their new knowledge into practice beyond the Shelburne Farms property.

sustainability throughout their curriculum and applying the knowledge and skills they need to improve their own schools and communities.

The complexity, scale, and urgency of issues we face today call for us to collaborate to increase our collective impact. Shelburne Farms works at multiple levels of scale with local, regional, state, national, and international programs. For decades we have supported networks of educators, schools, and other organizations. In 1999, we were a lead partner in launching the Education for Sustainability Project, a multiagency and grassroots campaign. The campaign resulted in Vermont being the first—and still only—state with sustainability as a public education standard. It also led Shelburne Farms to partner with the Burlington School District and the Bay and Paul Foundation to establish the Sustainability Academy at Lawrence Barnes School, the first sustainability-themed elementary school in the country.

Ten years ago, we helped pass the first Farm to School legislation in the country, designing a program for enabling children to have access to nutritious food, and creating new sales markets for local farmers. Teachers, food service staff, and students and their families learn where their food comes from, how it was grown, and how food choices affect health, the environment, the economy, and their communities.

For the last nine years, Shelburne Farms has served as the Northeast regional lead agency for the National Farm to School Network. Since 2006, we have supported the Farm-based Education Network, with 2,500 members from forty-eight states and twenty-eight countries. The network was established to strengthen and support the work of educators, farmers, and community leaders, and to provide access to experiences of all kinds on productive working farms. Over the past four decades, Shelburne Farms has engaged with partners on six continents to participate in global education for sustainability learning communities.

We invite you to join us on our journey at Shelburne Farms or in your own community, and be part of the shared vision of cultivating change for a sustainable future.

ACKNOWLEDGMENTS

Throughout the process of creating this book, I had the support of many individuals to whom I am deeply grateful.

At Shelburne Farms, I wish foremost to thank Alec Webb and Megan Camp for embracing this project and for the generosity they showed in providing me with access to the property and its welcoming staff during my many visits. I am also thankful to Alec for his thoughtful foreword and to Megan for her inspiring afterword. Their contributions provide personal perspectives on the decades that they, along with many others, helped to create a new vision for Shelburne Farms. Like many who have seen Shelburne Farms evolve, my gratitude also goes to Alec's brother, Marshall Webb, for his dedicated work to develop Shelburne Farms as a nonprofit organization.

Also at Shelburne Farms, several individuals offered valuable insight into their area of expertise that greatly informed the book's structure. For "Shelburne House," curator of collections Julie Eldridge Edwards provided thorough knowledge of its history; for "Formal Gardens," garden volunteer and former board of directors member Birgit Deeds shared her love and history of the gardens and their plantings; for "Farming the Land," dairy farm manager Sam Dixon explained the farm's operation and the care given for the animals' well-being; vegetable gardener Josh Carter welcomed us on countless trips to his beautiful and productive greenhouses and fields; and for "Farm-to-Table" and "Recipes," executive chef of the Inn at Shelburne Farms' restaurant James McCarthy provided both historical and contemporary interpretations of the role that food systems has played

PAGE 285
Handsome, leather-bound books line the shelves of Shelburne House's Library. More than six thousand of the Webbs' books remain in the Shelburne Farms Collections today.

PAGE 288
The interior ceiling of the Breeding Barn.

in preparing meals. I am particularly thankful for McCarthy's creations of outstanding farm- and garden-to-table dishes that have become recipes in this book. In addition, the amicable and energetic team of chefs, including Josh Fisher, Bill Beregi, Laura Miller, Kenny Bauer, and Meg Dawson, shared their knowledge about food preparation and cooking with fresh ingredients. Cheese operations manager Kate Turcote; cheese sales manager Rory Stamp; and maple syrup maker Dana Bishop shed light on Shelburne Farms' two important food products—Cheddar cheese and maple syrup. And finally, the Inn at Shelburne Farms' director, Hannah Sacco, was instrumental in coordinating productive and enjoyable visits to the property over the past year.

I am indebted to three resources that provided me with essential historical information about the Webb family and Shelburne Farms: *The History of Shelburne Farms: A Changing Landscape, An Evolving Vision* by Erica Hulyer Donnis; *Shelburne Farms: The History of an Agricultural Estate*, edited by William C. Lipke; and *Tour of the Inn at Shelburne Farms*, a reference document by Julie Eldridge Edwards. I highly recommend these publications to readers who are interested in learning more about the evolution of Shelburne Farms.

Ann Suokko served as liaison for our on-site work at Shelburne Farms. She also assisted with photography, transposed several interviews with Shelburne Farms' staff, and translated the food procedures for the "Recipes" chapter.

In New York, I wish to thank Rizzoli's senior editor Sandra Gilbert for encouraging me to create this book and for her excellent organization of this engaging project; associate publisher Margaret Rennolds Chace for her guidance; publisher, Charles Miers, for publishing the first major illustrated book on Shelburne Farms; and Hilary Ney and Elizabeth Smith for refining my prose.

Shelburne Farms opens its arms to many people of all ages from all over the world who engage in its beauty and gain experience and understanding from its educational, recreational, and cultural activities. I am thankful to the many trail walkers, restaurant diners, visiting families, schoolchildren, students, naturalists, food enthusiasts, and educators whom I have met or quietly observed over twenty-five years. Their enthusiasm and love for Shelburne Farms—a special place in the country—is truly moving.

NOTES

1   Tom Slayton, foreword to *The History of Shelburne Farms: A Changing Landscape, An Evolving Vision*, by Erica Huyler Donnis (Barre, VT: The Vermont Historical Society, and Shelburne, VT: Shelburne Farms, 2010), xii.

2   See National Park Service, National Historic Landmarks Program, https://www.nps.gov/nhl/.

3   Donnis, *The History of Shelburne Farms: A Changing Landscape, An Evolving Vision*, 35.

4   Ibid., 36.

5   Ibid., 95.

6   Ibid., 40.

7   Ibid., 17.

8   Shelburne Farms Archives. Lila Osgood Webb correspondence to E. F. Gebhardt, May 14, 1913, Farm Manager's Papers Collection, Box 3, Folder 23.

9   Birgit N. Deeds, *Shelburne Farms: A Guide to the Formal Gardens* (Shelburne, VT: Shelburne Farms, n.d.), 1.

10 Donnis, *The History of Shelburne Farms: A Changing Landscape, An Evolving Vision*, 80.

11 Ibid.

12 Deeds, *Shelburne Farms: A Guide to the Formal Gardens*, 7.

13 Donnis, *The History of Shelburne Farms: A Changing Landscape, An Evolving Vision*, 34.

14 William C. Lipke, ed., *Shelburne Farms: The History of an Agricultural Estate* (Burlington, VT: Robert Hull Fleming Museum, University of Vermont, 1979), 37.

15 Donnis, *The History of Shelburne Farms: A Changing Landscape, An Evolving Vision*, 70.

16 Ibid., 88.

17 Holly Brough, *Shelburne Farms: The Spirit of an Agricultural Estate* (Shelburne, VT: Shelburne Farms, 2011), 7.

18 Donnis, *The History of Shelburne Farms: A Changing Landscape, An Evolving Vision*, 55.

19 Ibid., 16.

20 Ibid., 61.

PHOTOGRAPHY CREDITS

All photographs copyright Glenn Suokko, with the exception of pages 26, 28, 30, 32, 62–63, 68, 70, 74, 76 (below), 84 (below), 88 (below), 92 (below), 94 (top), 100 (below), 102 (below), 104 (below), 116, 120, 146 (below), 152, 156, 162, 166, 168, 172, 176, 178, 186, 208, 228, 230, 232, endpapers, which are courtesy of Shelburne Farms Collections.

FRONT COVER
The Farm Barn is now the educational epicenter of Shelburne Farms.

ENDPAPERS
The circa-1922 panoramic photograph shows Shelburne House's Formal Gardens in their original glory. In the warmer months, the outdoor garden "rooms" were an extension of the house.

BACK COVER
The Formal Gardens at Shelburne House.

First published in the United States of America in 2017 by

Rizzoli International Publications, Inc.
300 Park Avenue South
New York, New York 10010
www.rizzoliusa.com

Text copyright ©2017 Glenn Suokko

All photography ©2017 Glenn Suokko, with the exception of photographs listed on left.

All rights reserved. No part of this publication may be reproduced, stored in a retrieval system, or transmitted in any form or by any means, electronic, mechanical, photocopying, recording, or otherwise, without prior consent of the publisher.

2017 2018 2019 2020 /10 9 8 7 6 5 4 3 2 1

Printed in China

ISBN 13: 978-0-8478-5884-2

Library of Congress Cataloging-in-Publication Data: 2016959902

Project Editor: Sandra Gilbert

Editorial Assistant provided by Hilary Ney, Elizabeth Smith, Rachel Selekman, and Deri Reed

Production Manager: Alyn Evans

Art Direction and Design: Glenn Suokko

Shelburne Farms
1611 Harbor Road
Shelburne, Vermont 05482
www.shelburnefarms.org